GENRE
FORMS OF DISCOURSE AND CULTURE

Volume 54, Number 2
July 2021

Big, Ambitious Novels
by Twenty-First-Century Women, Part 2
Edited by Courtney Jacobs and James Zeigler

Telling Stories That Never End:
Valeria Luiselli, the Refugee Crisis at the US-Mexico Border, and the Big, Ambitious Archival Novel

VALENTINA MONTERO ROMÁN

Mexican-born author Valeria Luiselli has published two projects focused on the twenty-first-century children's refugee crisis. The first, a book-length essay entitled *Tell Me How It Ends: An Essay in 40 Questions*, came out in 2017, and the second, a four-hundred-page novel called *Lost Children Archive*, was published in 2019. In interviews, Luiselli reveals that *Tell Me How It Ends* was supposed to be an addendum to *Lost Children Archive*, but she found herself unable to complete the novel until she published the essay on its own. The essay form, she says, was a more adequate "kind of vessel through which to express [her] political rage" (Berwick 2017). Despite this description, *Tell Me* contains an explanation for why Luiselli (2017: 96–97) might have felt the need to return to the novel:

> While the story [of the refugee crisis] continues, the only thing to do is tell it over and over again as it develops, bifurcates, knots around itself. And it must be told, because before anything can be understood, it has to be narrated many times, in many different words and from many different angles, by many different minds.

Lost Children is another angle, a different narration. It is also a "big, ambitious novel," one that mobilizes maximalist and encyclopedic narrative tendencies to confront the challenge of telling the knotty, bifurcating, ongoing story of the US-Mexico border crisis.

Scholarship has suggested that one of the strengths of encyclopedic fiction, one branch of the big, ambitious novel (BAN), is that it uses length and complexity to mimic "the nature of the encyclopedic enterprise itself—the audacious project of encompassing all that can be known within the covers of a book or

Genre, Vol. 54, No. 2   July 2021
DOI 10.1215/00166928-9263052   © 2021 by University of Oklahoma

books" (Clark 1992: 95). To evoke the encyclopedic is to pursue a project of "tentacular ambition . . . to pin down an entire writhing culture" (Wood 2001). In this essay, I suggest that Luiselli's novel offers us an opportunity to consider the archival as an alternative organizational principle for the BAN, one that offers a different historiography and an alternative epistemological orientation for the genre. A focus on the archival instead of the encyclopedic shifts attention from a pursuit of totality (and the inevitable limitations of such a project) to an exploration of the fragmented and recursive processes of constructing personal and historical memory. In this essay, I contend that Luiselli references the archive, instead of the encyclopedia, to represent the pervasive problems created by US racial construction—the subtle and not so subtle violences that resonate across time and space.[1] More specifically, I argue that the novel evokes the archive in its fragmentation, recombinant and recursive organization, and narrative multiplicity as a way to demonstrate the complexity and irreducibility of the refugee crisis and the constructions of Latinx difference that develop alongside it.[2]

The reference to the archive in *Lost Children Archive* reflects the novel's thematic focus on the nature of documentation as well as its formal experimentation. Ostensibly the story of a family on an "American" road trip, the novel describes a journey in which the characters explore the intersections of the histories of the Apache—pushed westward by Anglo-American settler colonialism—and the migrations of the children of the twenty-first-century US-Mexico border crisis. Each of the family members on the trip—an unnamed woman, her husband, and their two children, a five-year-old girl and a ten-year-old boy—pursues a curation project, collecting materials in a set of bankers boxes housed in the trunk of the car. The novel recounts the different documentational techniques the family uses to compile their "archives" and describes how they tell distinct stories about the materials they collect. The proliferation of materials referenced in their boxes

---

1. Marco Codebó (2007: 14) positions archival/dossier fiction as a form that reflects the "interactive, relational narratives of the digital era." In this essay, I offer another way of analyzing archival fiction by considering the genre in the context of feminist and critical race theory.

2. The terms *Latinx* and *people of color* refer to unstable constructions of identity that are complex and sometimes contradictory. Having said that, throughout this essay, I use the term *Latinx* when referring to a community of people who are of Latin American heritage. I also use it when I write about the ways Latinidad is constructed in the United States. For example, in this sentence, I use the term "Latinx difference" to signal a unique form of racial construction that Latin American people confront in the United States. I use the phrase "women and people of color" predominantly when I discuss or respond to scholarship that groups authors from historically marginalized communities together in order to explain their rarity in the history of the BAN.

and stories is mirrored at the level of form. *Lost Children* is an eclectic collection of narrative perspectives each of which provides a different approach to telling a story about "lost children." Besides the boxed materials that appear within the text, there are two first-person character-narrators, a third-person narrator in a novel-within-the-novel called *Lost Children Elegies*, and a series of citations, epigraphs, and allusions that produce a network of multimedial intertexts with their own documentational authority. Comprising fragmented, episodic chunks of narration interspersed with nonnumbered pages detailing the contents of the boxes, the novel evokes the archive in its layered organization and myriad narrative documents.

Lost Children creates a feeling of capaciousness and density through techniques often associated with the BAN, but the impact of those techniques is different. Indebted to a history of feminist thought in which mastery and synthetic totality are not the goal, Karla Holloway (2017: 774) points out that "the search for wholeness is representative of the critical strategies of Western cultures. It represents a sensibility that privileges the recovery of an individual (and independent) text over its fragmented textural dimensions." Luiselli's novel mobilizes maximalist tools to represent the unending project of accounting for the systems of marginalization that play out in discussions of the Latin American refugee crisis. Analyzing BAN narrative strategies like polyphony, fragmentation, and centripetal connectivity in the context of feminist, postcolonial, and critical race theory demonstrates that these techniques are the provenance of women and people of color at least as much as they are the domain of the white men often associated with the form. The difference is in recognizing that ambition can mean attentiveness to "fragmented textural dimensions" instead of mastery and synthetic totality. The archival organization of *Lost Children* connects the big, ambitious novel to theories of archival recovery, maximalism, and historical revision developed in feminist and critical race theory—from Saidiya Hartman's critical fabulation to Bharati Mukherjee's maximalist immigrant novel. Following these connections demonstrates an alternative history of the genre—one that reaches back not to Charles Dickens but to George Eliot and María Amparo Ruiz de Burton and not to James Joyce but to Jovita González, Virginia Woolf, and Zora Neale Hurston.

In section 1 of this essay, I reroute conceptualizations of the "ambition" of BAN's through a feminist and critical race reading of the form that refuses to reduce multiplicity in a pursuit of "mastery." In section 2, I analyze Luiselli's thematic focus on archival curation as a means for exploring the relationship between racialization and archival precarity, and in section 3, I argue that the novel's formal evocation of the archive is a tool for confronting the challenges of telling a knotty, unending story of racialized removals. The final section of the essay is an analysis that demonstrates how two specific aspects of Luiselli's big, ambitious archival novel cultivate an account of the refugee crisis that has a complex, discordant, recombinant structure that resists synthesis or simplification.

1. On Ambition: Systems and Universal Truths

Encyclopedic, maximalist, mega, and systems novels are all sometimes discussed under the umbrella of the "big, ambitious novel," but understanding what qualifies as a BAN is a complicated task. When James Wood (2000) coined the term to describe a genre of contemporary fiction, he did so by drawing parallels to the work of Charles Dickens, whose long novels he characterized as having the "ambition to describe all of society on its different levels." Scholars who have sought to explain what is ambitious about encyclopedic, maximalist, mega, and systems novels often similarly define ambition in relation to scale. Stefano Ercolino (2012: 243), for example, argues that the length of BANs is a result of "their ambition to realize synthetic-totalizing representations of the world." Similarly, in his history of the BAN, Mark Greif (2009: 29) contends that the ambition of 1970s mega-novels can be seen in the fact that their "ceaselessness of narration and proliferation of characters and plots revealed the domination of individual human lives by 'systems' with irresistible, superhuman logics: war in an age of technological rationality in *Gravity's Rainbow* or money in an age of finance capital in *JR*." Greif clarifies that

> "big, ambitious" books are big, not merely as a matter of pages, but as a feeling of spread, multifariousness, or open-endedness. They feel stuffed, overfull, or total; they feel longer than their straightforward story would require, and bigger than other books of similar length or complexity of plot. The books seem to have an aspiration to depict a state of American or global society that goes beyond the microcosm of a single family or the allegorization of a single "problem" within the American scene. (27)

BANs encourage readers to see, and possibly confront, the various national and global systems in which they are imbricated. What is ambitious about them is that they use their size to "understand and represent huge cultural realities" and reflect "on some of the most pressing questions of our time" (Ercolino 2014: 5, 10).

Although these accounts share an understanding of the value of size in the BAN, there are differences in how they articulate a history of the form. While Wood ties it to Dickens, Ercolino (2014: 26) suggests that the encyclopedism of maximalist novels is "rooted in the origins and at the heart of modernity, a genre that begins its course with Flaubert's *Bouvard et Pécuchet* [and] passes through modernism and James Joyce's *Ulysses*." For Greif (2009), the history of the BAN begins with two novels from the 1950s, Ralph Ellison's *Invisible Man* and Saul Bellow's *The Adventures of Augie March*. These varied historical contexts emerge as disparate points of view because they attend to different qualities of the BAN. Dickens's flat characters immersed in a web of connections speak to Wood's conceptualization of "paranoid," hysterical realism; the totalizing effects of Joyce's representation of Dublin correspond to what Ercolino (2014: 26) describes as the BAN's encyclopedism and diegetic exuberance; and the "interminability of narration" and "unending profligacy" (Greif 2009: 24) of Ellison and Bellow are Greif's precursors to the BAN as "perpetual-motion machine" (Wood 2000).

Regardless of the history they describe, each of these accounts implies that there are very few women and people of color who have produced these kinds of big, ambitious novels. Despite the fact that Greif (2009: 28, 27) begins his analysis with novels that explore "race and the escape from history in *Invisible Man*, and race and upward mobility in *Augie March*," he suggests that the BAN "passes back out of the hands of black and Jewish writers (and never passes into the hands of women writers), to be restored to practitioners who are white Protestant men (Pynchon, Gaddis)." Greif does not explicitly provide a logic for why this happens, but Ercolino (2014), who seeks to explain his analysis of a fairly homogenous set of maximalist authors, reaches back to the work of Tom LeClair (1989) to explain the dearth of women and people of color in its history.

LeClair's monograph, published in 1989, argues that systems novels are texts that "master—comprehend, represent, and critique—the world, for the world, as systems theorists recognize, is largely composed of huge systems of information, both ideological and institutional, that exert power over individuals and their groups" (14). He contends that women and people of color are rarely included in this history because they have been "deprived of full participation in American life" and have subsequently been unable to access the "white male's luxury of examining the whole of American or multinational culture from within, from the perspective of full membership" (29). Although he says he teaches authors like

Leslie Marmon Silko and Ishmael Reed as novelists that can critique a dominant culture and propose an alternative, he does not believe they produce texts that "master the power systems of America as thoroughly or profoundly as the books" he studies as systems novels (30).

LeClair suggests that women and people of color do not fit into his definition of mastery "at a formal or stylistic level," because they write from an "outsider's view" that is only "valuable to her or his group" (30). In his view, novels by historically marginalized authors are unable to do what systems novels do: "to solicit and transform the reader's interests, to shift his or her attention from the personal and local to the communal and global" (3). Using Alice Walker as an example, he argues that though *The Color Purple* may be more "culturally significant to black women readers," Thomas Pynchon's *Gravity's Rainbow* "masters a set of global conditions that *The Color Purple* does not address, conditions and systems in which *all readers*—black or white, female or male, old or young—are imbricated" (3; emphasis added). Later he contends something similar about Toni Morrison, asserting that "Morrison does not examine how her people share with *all people* subjugation by various kinds of national and transnational power systems" (30; emphasis added). In both of these examples, the rationale for why the writing of Black women authors should not be considered in his analysis of mastery is that their work does not speak to systems that *all readers* experience.

LeClair's arguments demonstrate the pervasive idea that writing by women and people of color is niche and thus unable to address issues that impact a global or national community. Though his monograph is now over a quarter century old, his arguments still circulate in discussions of the history of the BAN. Even as late as 2014, Stefano Ercolino's (2014: 10) analysis of maximalist novels contends that though LeClair's argument "can be debated . . . it is probably true." The logic employed by Ercolino and LeClair implies that the reason for the scarcity of BAN's by women and people of color is that historically marginalized people have not produced novels that seek to "understand and represent huge cultural realities" (LeClair 1989: 31). Claims like LeClair's suggest that to write from a position of whiteness is to write from a position that is neutral and thus more readily "concerned with exerting influence over the culture as a whole rather than with finding a niche in the literary canon" (18). Such lines of argumentation also do not consider systems of racial and gender oppression as a part of the large cultural wholes that are of interest to BANs. When work by women or people of color is included in the history of the genre, it is often positioned as an exception, a token, or, as is the case for Wood (2000), a convenient focalizer for a critique of the genre as a whole. In this essay, though, I argue that if ambition is the ability to "comprehend, represent, and critique the . . . huge systems of information, both ideological and institutional, that exert power over individuals and their groups," then there are indisputably women and people of color who have used narrative ambitiously, particularly in their attempts to comprehend, represent, and critique racism, sexism, and colonialism—systems that both engender the capitalist and "technological rationality" often marked as the appropriate fodder of BANs and that impact *all* people across race, gender, ability, nationality, and sexuality.

2. On Archives: Who Gets Documented

In this section, I analyze Luiselli's thematic interest in the archive in order to explain the ambition of her formal experimentation with BAN narrative techniques. The title of *Lost Children* marks it as an "archive" but within the context of the novel the meaning of that word is just as abstruse as it was when Jacques Derrida (1995: 90) suggested that "nothing is less clear . . . than the word 'archive.'" Marlene Manoff (2004: 10) points out that an archive can be all of "the contents of museums, libraries, and archives and thus the entire extant historical record," or it can be "a small subset of . . . material, typically a discrete collection of related . . . documents." In the novel, the most prominent discussion of archives surrounds the seven bankers boxes the family has brought with them on their trip from New York City to Echo Canyon in Arizona's Chiricahua Mountains. Four of the boxes belong to the husband, who is working on a soundscape project he describes as "an inventory of echoes" centered on "the ghosts of Geronimo and the Apaches" (Luiselli 2019: 21). One box belongs to the woman narrator and contains the materials for a sound project focused on the refugee crisis, a project she begins after working with a Mixteca woman named Manuela who is looking for her two daughters.[3] The remaining two boxes are for each of the children to fill as they travel across the country. The characters collect photographs, maps, postcards, sound recordings, and notes as well as journals and books, and the woman narrator explicitly calls the boxes an archive, though she notes that it may be "optimistic to call [their] collected mess an archive" (42). The titular "archive"

---

3. Manuela's daughters were denied asylum and disappeared while being transferred from a detention center.

of *Lost Children* could be the materials collected by the family, but it could also be the sum of the various documentations developed throughout the text. As I pointed out at the beginning of this essay, the novel itself is a "small subset of materials," a repository of documents that draws attention to the silences and elisions of historical memory.

The proliferating archive(s) of *Lost Children* highlight the myopia of dominant historiography in ways that intersect with archival scholarship. The International Council on Archives defines archives as spaces that "constitute the memory of nations and of societies, shape their identity, and [serve as the] cornerstone of the information society" (quoted in Lazo 2010: 36). As Rodrigo Lazo explains, archives are "inextricable from the establishment of nation-states" (36). They reflect the way power dictates historical memory. Moreover, as Derrida's (1995: 4) oft-cited footnote suggests, "There is no political power without control of the archive, if not memory. Effective democratization can always be measured by this essential criterion: the participation in and access to the archive, its constitution, and its interpretation." In both form and content, Luiselli's novel considers this connection between archival construction, historical memory, and political power.

Long before we had theoretical frameworks for the correspondence between democratization and archival inclusion, women and people of color sought to correct their elision and misrepresentation in the national imaginary. In both fiction and nonfiction, women across racial and ethnic difference worked to address archival myopia through storytelling. In the nineteenth and twentieth centuries, for example, authors as diverse as María Amparo Ruiz de Burton, George Eliot, Zora Neale Hurston, Ella Deloria, Virginia Woolf, Edith Eaton, Dorothy Richardson, and Jovita González wrote fiction that unsettled the construction of cultural and historical memory about their various communities.[4] They experimented

---

4. There is, of course, a much more expansive genealogy of authors that could be mentioned here, but I have provided a few meaningful examples. Hurston dedicated her life to producing fiction, anthropology, and folklore that undermined eugenics science and complicated well-trodden racist and sexist stereotypes. Folklore scholar Jovita González produced fiction and nonfiction that revised Texas history as an Anglo invasion of the borderlands. Virginia Woolf wrote about women's misrepresentation across genres. "Woman," she wrote, "is all but absent from history," the product of not having the material conditions to produce her own stories and histories: "In real life she could hardly read, could scarcely spell, and was the property of her husband" (Woolf 1929: 43). In recent years, authors from Julia Alvarez, Helena Maria Viramontes, and Ana Castillo to Dahlma Llanos-Figueroa and Carmen Maria Machado have built from this history, using literature to correct dominant historical narratives and revise national and cultural mythologies.

with stream of consciousness and free indirect discourse, with historical fiction, the short story, and the autofictional essay in ways that pushed back against histories that sought to exclude them. Indeed, many of the narrative qualities associated with the BAN—ambition, fragmentation, recursivity, interminable narration, and polyphony—can be seen in their work.

Lost Children undoubtedly deserves to be considered as part of a genealogy of texts that ameliorate the unheard accounts of historically marginalized communities, but it is also a novel that uses an evocation of the archive to highlight the conditions through which stories are repressed or erased in the first place. In the woman narrator's account (which takes up roughly the first half of the novel), the personal archive of the family becomes a space for considering the power-based distortions of dominant archives and notions of belonging. Her reflections on the photographs, maps, postcards, sound recordings, journals, and books of their collection create a foundation for imagining the utility of a proliferation of documentary techniques and archival constructions, an exigency to which the archival form of the novel responds.

Analyzing how the archive functions thematically in *Lost Children* is a useful way for understanding the significance of the novel's archival form. The woman's research highlights how the racialization of Latinx people results in their "removal" both from notions of citizenship and from historical archives. Describing one article that says Latinx refugees are from "mostly poor and violent towns," she argues that the subtext of this characterization is that refugee children come from a "barbaric reality" and are "most probably, not white" (Luiselli 2019: 50). Similarly, after encountering a piece that describes a "Biblical Plague" of "illegal aliens" carrying disease into the country, the woman contends that the article's portrayal supports a "convenient narrative" that Latinx people are a "barbaric periphery whose chaos and brownness threaten civilized white peace" (124). "Only such a narrative," she says, "can justify decades of dirty war, interventionist policies, and the overall delusion of moral and cultural superiority of the world's economic and military powers" (124).

For the woman narrator, media coverage that racializes Latinx refugees contributes to a national narrative that dictates who belongs in this country and whose stories are included in the archive of "American" history. Throughout the novel, she outlines a relationship between racialized "removals" and archival marginalization. For example, her box contains a loose note that posits euphemisms as a means for distorting historical records and obscuring histories of oppression:

Euphemisms hide, erase, coat.

Euphemisms lead us to tolerate the unacceptable. And, eventually, to forget.

Against a Euphemism, remembrance. In order to not repeat. Remember terms and meanings. Their absurd disjointedness.

Term: *Our Peculiar Institution*. Meaning: slavery (Epitome of all euphemisms.)

Term: *Removal*. Meaning: expulsion and dispossession of people from their lands. . . .

Term: *Relocation*. Meaning: confining people in reservations.

Term: *Reservation*. Meaning: a wasteland, a sentence to perpetual poverty.

Term: *Removal*. Meaning: expulsion of people seeking refuge.

Term: *Undocumented*. Meaning: people who will be removed. (Luiselli 2019: 255–56)

The euphemisms listed here suggest that being removed from notions of belonging and citizenship also means geographical relocation and elision from the historical archive. The note marks euphemisms as a part of a process of marginalization that Natalia Molina (2018) calls "relational racism": a mobilization of "racial scripts" that mark people as "other" through recurrent narratives of difference. Racial scripts designate certain communities as less intelligent, disease-ridden, and more prone to violence and hypersexuality in order to argue against their suffrage, citizenship, and humanity. The woman's note draws attention to the fact that those ideas are "built into institutional structures and practices that form society's 'scaffolding,' like laws and policies" (Molina 2018: 103) in ways that are then euphemistically effaced in historical record. Euphemisms reflect a mobilization of racial scripts that results in geographical relocation, removal from narratives of belonging, and disappearance from the archive of national history.[5]

The connection between racialized removal and documentational elision begins on the first pages of the novel and highlights the way the novel posits the need for recursive attention to archival absences. The text opens with a pair of epigraphs:

An archive presupposes an archivist, a hand that collects and classifies.
—Arlette Farge

---

5. Molina (2014: 5) points out that although racialized groups experience racism and discrimination in ways that "are varied and can pivot along lines of citizenship, class, language, gender, and sexuality," racial scripts demonstrate that "society is predisposed (consciously or not) to utilize historical experience and stereotypes of past groups to define and circumscribe the place and role of future members of U.S. society" (16). A relational analysis attends to the ways racism connects people across disparate groups despite their different experiences of that system of oppression. Luiselli's woman narrator highlights the ways relational racism has shaped the US-Mexico border crisis, but that does not mean that we should understand that process as erasing or minimizing the distinct and often uneven consequences of relational racism in the United States.

To leave is to die a little.
To arrive is never to arrive.
　—Migrant prayer (Luiselli 2019: 3)

Framing the section titled "Relocations," these excerpts serve as a provocation to consider the relocations and elisions of archival construction as resonant with the deportations and disappearances of migrants and refugees. Luiselli's excision of two lines from the migrant's prayer effaces the more religious meaning of the aggregate text in which migration is framed as a movement toward God. The decontextualized fragment suggests a less uplifting understanding of what it means to relocate: for refugees, movement from one place to another entails leaving a previous life with only a tenuous understanding of what it will mean to arrive in the United States. As the woman narrator describes it, a refugee is

> someone who has already arrived somewhere, in a foreign land, but must wait for an indefinite time before actually, fully having arrived. Refugees wait in detention centers, shelters, or camps; in federal custody and under the gaze of armed officials. They wait in long lines for lunch, for a bed to sleep in, wait with their hands raised to ask if they can use the bathroom. . . . They wait for visas, documents, permission. (Luiselli 2019: 47–48)

And sometimes they never fully arrive. They become dots on the mortality maps that the woman collects in her box, arriving in the United States "officially" only when they have died.

The woman chooses to shift her attention to refugees who never "arrive" as a response to her concerns about archival precarity.[6] In focusing on "the children who are missing, those whose voices can no longer be heard because they are, possibly forever, lost" (Luiselli 2019: 146), the woman's research explores what Rodrigo Lazo (2010: 37–38) might characterize as migrant archives, archives that "reside in obscurity and are always at the edge of annihilation," containing texts "that have not been written into the official spaces of archivization, even though they weave in and out of the buildings that house documents." Working to account for people whose lives only become visible in the documents that record their disappearances and deaths means making visible the fact that those documents are "little more than a register of [their] encounter with power," accounts that provide only "a meager sketch of [their] existence" (Hartman 2008:

---

6. It is also a reflection of her worries about how to create an ethical and meaningful account of the refugee crisis. Although she says that "a valuable archive of the refugee crisis would need to be composed, fundamentally, of a series of testimonies or oral histories that register their own voices telling their stories," the woman narrator decides that she does not think it is right to turn the lives of child refugees "into material for media consumption" (Luiselli 2019: 96).

2).[7] It means telling what Saidiya Hartman calls "impossible stories"—stories that pursue the "impossible goal [of] redressing the violence that produced numbers, ciphers, and fragments of discourse" in the dominant archive by "embody[ing] life in words and at the same time respect[ing] what we cannot know" (2).

The first half of *Lost Children* follows the woman narrator's anxious ruminations about how to create a process of remembrance that calls attention to the expulsion, dispossession, and violence that euphemisms and removals conceal. In the end, though, we never get an answer about the shape her final project takes. Instead, her recursive attention to the bankers box archives and the novel's transition to a new character narrator indicate the text's commitment to revision, recombination, and repetition as crucial tools for narrating impossible stories. In the second half of the novel, the boy takes narrative control, offering another account of the events of the road trip and highlighting the fact that the woman's metadiscursive reflections on archival curation frame the novel's formal experimentation with documentational accretion. In the next section of this essay, I outline the ways the novel's archival form amplifies the processes of remembrance the woman narrator pursues so that, in both content and structure, the text insists on the importance of continuing to note when and where power produces erasure.

3. On Form: How to Tell Impossible Stories

As the woman narrator works to tell a story about refugees who never fully arrive, either in the archive or in the United States, her concerns about the best way to create a sound project are the means through which the novel articulates archival curation as its central formal innovation. The archive is repeatedly marked as a source of inspiration, a space comprising layered documents that enable myriad interpretations even as they produce inevitable elisions and a proliferation of

---

7. In her essay, "Venus in Two Acts," Hartman (2008) describes how the archive of Atlantic slavery represents Venus. She contends that though "she is found everywhere in the Atlantic world" (1) no one "remembered her name or recorded the things she said, or observed that she refused to say anything at all" (2). Hartman reflects on power and documentation by paraphrasing ideas from Foucault's essay "Lives of Infamous Men." Foucault (2003: 284) focuses on texts from the seventeenth and eighteenth centuries, but Hartman builds from his argument that archive fragments "survive only from the clash with a power that wished only to annihilate them or at least to obliterate them." Though Foucault is discussing a particular historical moment and form of documentation, Hartman's work highlights the utility of understanding that the lives attached to archival documents "can no longer be separated out from the declamations, the tactical biases, the obligatory lies that power games and power relations presuppose" (Foucault 2003: 282).

echoes. Unlike a "proper story," which, as Luiselli's woman narrator understands it, must have "a beginning, a middle, and an end," an archive is a repository that houses information that can be reorganized and shuffled into different arrangements. It has a different temporality because it can be added to and reorganized in ways that can alter salient themes and information.[8]

Lost Children's discussions of the utility of archival curation play out in the novel's organization. While "shuffling around" in the boxes in the back of the car, the woman narrator thinks that "by trying to listen to all the sounds trapped in the archive, [she] might find a way into the exact story [she] needs to document, the exact form it needs" (Luiselli 2019: 42).[9] She believes that in "reading others' words, inhabiting their minds for a while," she might find an entry point into her own sound project (57). Sifting through the archive, though, also highlights for her "what any other mind might do with the same collection of bits and scraps, now temporarily archived in a given order in those boxes. How many possible combinations of all those documents were there? And what completely different stories would be told by their varying permutations, shufflings, and reorderings?" (57). The novel enacts its own shuffling and reordering by providing multiple accounts of the bankers box materials. The woman narrator provides one story about the trip and documents, and the boy contributes another. Moreover, the novel depicts the contents of the boxes in nonnarrative space, allowing for unnarrated details to circulate in conversation with the accounts given by the character narrators and authorizing alternative explanations of the projects and materials the characters discuss.

The fragmented construction of *Lost Children* allows for the possibility of imagining an archival fiction whose contents can be added to and reorganized. The novel comprises four main parts ("Family Soundscape," "Reenactment," "Apacheria," and "Lost Children Archive") that are each a combination of fragmented, episodic chunks of narration interspersed with nonnumbered pages that depict the contents of the bankers boxes. The first part of the novel, "Family Soundscape," for example, breaks down in the following way:

---

8. Archives, as Codebó (2007: 9) points out, are collections of materials that allow researchers to "determine their own path of inquiry."

9. Because the woman narrator and her husband are both working on sound projects, the novel's exploration of the archive often uses language and conceptual tools from sound studies. For example, the woman narrator suggests that gaps and fragmentation in archives might be understood as "sound rubble, noise, and debris" (29). You can see more of how sound shapes the woman narrator's conceptualization of the archive in some of the quotes recorded in section 3 of this essay. Though there is no room to expand here, this aspect of the novel would benefit from analysis in the context of theories of sound and the archive.

Relocations
Box I
Routes and Roots
Box II
Undocumented
Box III
Missing
Box IV
Removals

"Relocations," which is about thirty pages long, has twenty-one episodic seg-
ments with subheadings like "Inventory," "Itemization," "Joint Filing," "Foundational Myths," "Mother Tongues," "Time," "Teeth," and "Tongue Ties." This seg-
mentation continues throughout the novel, creating an abundance of narrative and
nonnarrative documents that can be imagined as "a collection of bits and scraps"
only "temporarily archived in a given order." The sense that a reorganization of
the pieces could provide a different permutation of the story is substantiated when
subheadings and citations recirculate in different narrative accounts, deployed
in different sequences and containing seemingly unrelated details. "Time" and
"Teeth" from the woman's account, for example, become "Time & Teeth" in the
boy's.

The novel's form refuses to propose a stable story with a beginning, middle,
and end. As Luiselli (2017: 97) notes in *Tell Me How It Ends*, the story of refugee children is one that needs to be retold "over and over again as it develops,
bifurcates, knots around itself"; it is a story about ongoing systemic oppression
that should be consistently revisited and revised from different perspectives
and in different mediums to combat historical amnesia. As the woman narrator describes it, documentation—the process of accounting "for something, an
object, our lives, or a story" through "the lens of a camera, on paper, or with a
sound recording device"—is "only a way of contributing one more layer, something like soot, to all the things already sedimented in a collective understanding
of the world" (Luiselli 2019: 55). In this context, the novel's archival form can be
imagined as a method for contributing to an accretion of meaning that develops
through recursive attention—through relocations and shufflings.

The sedimentation of stories available within this archival novel, though,
does not aim to "give voice" to those who are absent in the archive; the proliferation of narrative perspectives highlights instead of minimizes the absent stories

---

10. Hartman's work is helpful in thinking about this strategy. She suggests that narratives that
address inadequate archives aim "not to *give voice* . . . but rather to imagine what cannot be verified,

of refugees.[10] Throughout her work, the woman narrator comes to believe that the only way to tell a story of the refugees who never "arrive" is to look for the reverberations, echoes, and resonances that their absences create. Reflecting on the research anthropologist Steven Feld did on the Bosavi of Papua New Guinea, the woman notes that echoes can be understood as "gone reverberations," which are "an absence turned into presence; and, at the same time . . . a presence that [makes] an absence audible" (Luiselli 2019: 98). She comes to understand that she and her husband are working on similar projects, creating an "inventory of echoes" that are "not a collection of sounds that have been lost—such a thing would in fact be impossible—but rather one of sounds that were present in the time of recording and that, when we listen to them, remind us of the ones that are lost" (141). The woman narrator's research highlights the missing narratives of the refugees by collecting material records that account for their absence.

Luiselli's focus on archival curation as a means for telling a story about the refugee crisis can be positioned productively alongside scholarship in postcolonial, feminist, and critical race theory that has thought extensively about how to navigate the hole-riddled histories of marginalized groups. In her influential work on Black intimate life in the early twentieth century, Saidiya Hartman (2020) articulates the challenges historians face in navigating flawed archives. She contends that "every historian of the multitude, the dispossessed, the subaltern, and the enslaved is forced to grapple with the power and authority of the archive and the limits it sets on what can be known, whose perspective matters, and who is endowed with the gravity and authority of historical actor" (Hartman 2020: xiii). Hartman's (2008: 12) method for intervening in this space is a practice of critical fabulation that can "say what resists being said" and create "a history of an unrecoverable past, . . . a narrative of what might have been or could have been . . . written with and against the archive." Although narration can never "exceed the limits of the sayable dictated by the archive," a process of critical fabulation demonstrates that documentation that relegates marginalized people to dots and blurbs can be "elaborate[d], augment[ed], [and] transpose[d]" (Hartman 2020: xiv).

While Luiselli's big, ambitious archival novel is not what Hartman would

---

a realm of experience which is situated between two zones of death—social and corporeal death—and to reckon with the precarious lives which are visible only in the moment of their disappearance." This work requires "listening for the unsaid, translating misconstrued words, and refashioning disfigured lives" (Hartman 2008: 12).

describe as critical fabulation, *Lost Children* is an analogous attempt at using narrative experimentation to tell an impossible story. Layering different documentation techniques and dispersing thematic threads through multiple controlling "archivists," the novel suggests that the limitations of archival curation mandate recursivity as a strategy for narrating an ongoing story. This approach simultaneously highlights and ameliorates archival precarity. Moreover, it demonstrates how the echoes and reverberations of a recursive and referential narrative form can be made meaningful as spaces of remembrance.

The archival form Luiselli deploys to create a knotty, recursive process of remembrance resonates with discussions of memory and the archive in Chicana feminist studies. In discussing the absence of Chicana feminist genealogies, Maylei Blackwell (2011: 11) points out that "exclusionary historical narratives do not merely *represent* historical realities but help to produce those realities by enforcing the boundaries of legitimate political memory and the subjectivities they authorize." Blackwell's delineation of the fact that dominant archives produce the historical marginalization that they record highlights the constructedness of memory. Documentation does not just record what was or is there, it also creates structures for knowing that which was previously unknown and provides frameworks for what can be imagined and produced. Because of this, counterhistories and the pursuit of what she describes as "retrofitted memory" can offer new horizons of possibility (Blackwell 2011: 11).

In *Lost Children*, the process of remembrance the woman narrator discusses is attuned to the productive tension "between document and fabrication," between a lived experience of the past and the documents that create their own memories (Luiselli 2019: 42). Echoes and reverberations are not a direct account of lived experience, but they provide what the woman narrator calls "borrowed memories" that can prevent historical amnesia. She describes one way to imagine a translation of story to shared, communal memory when she decides to read the experimental novel *Lost Children Elegies* aloud, noting that moving from "the ink lines of the page" to the sound of spoken words culminates in a conversion of "impressions, images, future borrowed memories" (144). Later, the boy describes another version of the impact of documentation when he narrates his experience photographing a plane of deported refugee children in this way: "As I tucked the picture back in between some pages toward the end of the book, I realized something important, which is this: that everything that happened after I took the picture was also inside it, even though no one could see it, except me when I looked at it, and maybe also you, in the future, when you look at it, even if you didn't even see the original moment with your own eyes" (200). The systems of remembrance that Luiselli and Blackwell describe highlight the constructed nature of personal and historical memory in ways that allow documents like photographs, historical accounts, and novels to function as tools for altering not just the way we view the past but the way we can experience the present and imagine the future. The act of documenting erasure, silence, and reverberation does not simply insert marginalized people into histories from which they have been effaced; instead, moving "within the gaps, interstices, silences, and crevices of the uneven narratives of domination" generates possibilities "for fracturing dominant narratives and creating spaces for new historical subjects to emerge" (Blackwell 2011: 2–3).

Like critical fabulations, retrofitted and borrowed memories highlight "the mechanics of erasure in historical writing" and "undermine, instead of replicate, the power relations and regimes of truth that hold these mechanics in place" (Blackwell 2011: 3, 4). But telling a story that highlights those systems of power means attending to the limitations of traditional narrative forms. As Emma Pérez (1999: xiv) points out, "The systems of thought which have patterned our social and political institutions, our universities, our archives, and our homes predispose us to a predictable beginning, middle, and end to untold stories." The only way to undermine the structures of thought inherent in dominant historiography—the only way to embrace what Pérez calls the "decolonial imaginary"—is to move away from that story form. In this context, Luiselli's use of BAN strategies that focus on "that which is different, fragmented, imagined, non-linear, non-teleological" (Pérez 1999: xiv) does not demonstrate an encyclopedic goal of making visible the "illusory basis of 'total knowledge'" (Herman 2010: 137) or the "ever more voluminous and unmanageable, information" of our contemporary moment (Letzler 2012: 8). Instead, the knotty, bifurcating form of Luiselli's BAN highlights the systems of power that decide whose knowledge and stories matter in the ongoing accretion of national and historical memory. Luiselli's mobilization of BAN techniques demonstrates what Blackwell (2011: 11) calls a process of "re-membering" and what Luiselli's (2019: 174) woman narrator describes as "re-cognizing," a system of remembrance that highlights alternative histories and the decolonial imaginaries that they might allow.

4. On Genre: The Affordances of Archival Fiction

Lost Children raises the issues of exclusion noted in archival discourse while also demonstrating how the gaps and silences of archives can generate echoes and resonances that might serve as a valuable account of the complexity of the refugee crisis and its documentation. In this section, I explore the affordances of the big, ambitious archival novel, developing, in particular, two meaningful contexts for the form: immigrant maximalism and archive fever.

Immigrant Maximalism

As I mentioned earlier, *Lost Children* is a novel that contains varied narrative perspectives and forms. The text has two first-person character narrators, a third-person narrator in an experimental novel-within-the-novel, images of documented materials, song transcripts, and numerous references and citations. In collecting these disparate texts, the archive of the novel complicates any singular account while also querying the values and limitations of different mediums, perspectives, and genres (sound vs. image vs. text, third-person vs. first-person narration, etc.). In a reading of BANs like Ercolino's (2012: 247), the polyphony of *Lost Children* might be understood as a tool for placing "every type of individual, or individualizing instance, in a subordinate position" in ways that evoke LeClair's (1989: 14) conceptualization of a world in which systems "exert power over individuals and their groups." But instead of a "hierarchically horizontal" organization that "demonstrates that it is not the single individual, or the single story, that matters . . . but rather a collective of characters and a plurality of stories" (Ercolino 2012: 246), the polyphony of *Lost Children* suggests the importance of each distinct individual story, especially those that are destroyed or silenced. Although *Lost Children* contains an abundance of narrative perspectives, the archival form does not create a totalizing representation in which everyone is dominated in a horizontal manner. Instead, the novel's organization suggests a more nuanced representation of systemic oppression, a response that is best understood in relationship to long-standing feminist theorizations of multiplicity and maximalism.

In 1988, Bharati Mukherjee argued that minimalism was a technique that was "designed to keep out anyone with too much story to tell" (28). She wanted immigrant novelists to embrace maximalism so they could fill the world with characters that were "bursting with stories, too many to begin telling" and characters who had "lived through centuries of history in a single lifetime" (28). Mukherjee suggests that maximalism offers immigrant authors the space necessary to represent an endless proliferation of narratives that speak to "the biggest stories in recent American history" (28).

In the context of Mukherjee's conceptualization of maximalism, the hypertrophy of a text like Luiselli's speaks to the importance of what philosopher Maria Lugones (2010: 755) describes as the maintenance of "multiplicity at the point of reduction—not in maintaining a hybrid 'product,' which hides the colonial difference—in the tense workings of more than one logic, not to be synthesized but transcended." Narrative proliferation maintains a multiplicity not to represent a synthetic totality but to highlight variegated stories and logics. Maximalist multiplicity can thus be understood in terms of Chela Sandoval's (1991: 14) articulation of oppositional consciousness, a denial of "any one ideology as the final answer," a representational technique that "posit[s] a tactical subjectivity with the capacity to recenter depending upon the kinds of oppression to be confronted." In this context, narrative profusion becomes a means for navigating the endlessly mutable systems of racial construction that maintain oppressive hierarchies.

In the work of an author like Luiselli, multiplicity and fragmentation do not create a "neutral diegetic organization" (Ercolino 2012: 246), and they do not suggest that all stories have the same weight within the context of the novel. One of the benefits of a heterogeneous, proliferating, hypertrophic archive is that it suggests that depicting "big cultural realities" that impact "everyone" does not mean that everyone's story is the same under any given systemic logic or even under any given identity category. *Lost Children* highlights a distinction between the woman narrator—who is documented, racially ambiguous, and a part of the intellectual class—and the Latinx people who are most vulnerable to the immigration policies of the United States—people who are racialized because of their "barbaric" origins, skin color, language proficiency, class, or educational background. The novel tells us that the woman was born in Mexico (Luiselli 2019: 129) and that her grandmother was Hñähñu (16), her father was a Mexican diplomat, and her mother was a part of a guerilla movement in southern Mexico (173), but we do not get an account of her relationship to the immigration system of the United States other than that she and her husband are able to show border patrol substantiating documentation. While the text notes her experiences of racialization in moments where responses to her accent and to her place of birth fall in a range between uncomfortable and threatening, those moments of discomfort and fear are made meaningful through their alignment and divergence from the accounts she gives of the migrant crisis and its historical connection to other forms of racial violence.[11] *Lost Children* demonstrates that the construction of racial difference (through the explication of the category of "Latino/a/x") can result in both the social censure and racial profiling that the family experiences and the disappearances, deportations, and deaths that the woman documents in her work. However, it also signals the incommensurability of those experiences.

The fragmentation and polyphony of Luiselli's immigrant maximalist novel makes visible the varied ways racial construction impacts people across difference instead of suggesting that all individuals experience being subsumed in global and national systems in horizontally impactful ways. Formally, this plays out in the way narrative space is allocated throughout the text. The documents that are the only records of refugee arrival are hole-riddled maps and narrative fragments, while the stories collected by the woman and boy narrator—the texts that produce echoes and highlight refugee absence—are circulated, read, and cited repeatedly. That is, even though the archival form of the novel amends dominant, Anglo constructions of history that relegate refugees to the margins, the novel still represents the power distinctions that dictate who can and cannot create and maintain archives. There is no reduction of the uneven distributions of power (and thus narrative space) that correspond to racialized notions of citizenship and belonging. In *Lost Children*, the proliferation of accounts—its fragmentation and recursivity, its pursuit of myriad stories about lost children, and its inclusion of heterogeneous narrators and documentations—creates an immigrant maximalist archival novel that does not assert a unified experience of racialization in the United States or in the pursuit of citizenship.[12]

---

11. The woman says, for example, that "in a town called Loco," she gets asked about her accent and place of birth, and when she answers the response is "just cold, dead silence, as if [she's] confessed a sin" (Luiselli 2019: 129). She also describes nervousness when presenting passports to the border patrol (129) and fear when the family flees a man's house in the borderlands (132). However, these incidents are held in tension with her description of the experiences of communities of Indigenous and Afro-Indigenous Latinx people. At a protest the woman narrator attends, the majority of people who have had family disappear during ICE raids are Afro-Indigenous Garifuna from Honduras (115). Likewise, the woman narrator's work with Manuela, a Mixteca woman, is organized around trying to find her daughters. At the end of the novel, we learn that they are dead (349). Some reviewers have critiqued the ways the text marks similarities between the woman narrator's children and Manuela's, but, although the novel does explore this connection, I think there is value in an analysis that acknowledges the ways the archival form and thematic focus of the novel make visible the distinctions between the two families as well as their connections.

12. It seems important to note that the novel's focus on echoes means that it does not center narratives by Black or Indigenous people, even when that might be expected (as with the husband's

Not Paranoid or Hysterical, but Feverish

One of the unifying features attributed to big, ambitious novels is that they have a totalizing aim or a thematic arc that results in centripetal connectivity. As Wood describes it in his discussion of what he calls the hysterical realism of the BAN, "The different stories all intertwine, and double and triple on themselves. Characters are forever seeing connections and links and plots, and paranoid parallels." For Wood (2000), "There is something essentially paranoid about the belief that everything is connected to everything else" in "an endless web." Ercolino (2014: 250) elaborates on Wood's argument, suggesting that the paranoid concerns of maximalist novels are "often a question of hypothetical threats" that are "impossible to demonstrate and at times absolutely implausible or ridiculous."

To read the accretion of layered narrative arcs and documentational methods in *Lost Children* within the paradigm of paranoid connectivity would be a mistake because it would minimize the novel's depiction of the recurrent patterns identifiable in histories of racial violence and refugee crises. The connections, links, and plots of this novel are not implausible or ridiculous. So, instead of a paranoid imagination, I would like to propose that this novel depicts a feverish one, overwhelmed and inundated by the project of remembering and recounting the histories of erasure and violence that connect to the story of child refugees. The webs of connection in this novel evoke how it feels to navigate an archive of the stories and histories, documentations and maps, ghosts and ephemera that dictate humanity and citizenship as well as presence and arrival in the United States.

Luiselli's novel has a citational density and palimpsest-like organization that mirrors and expands, at the level of narrative form, the woman narrator's experience of research and archival curation. The woman describes her archive as a "documental labyrinth of [her] own making" that culminates in "long sleepless nights reading about archive fevers, about rebuilding memory in diasporic narratives, about being lost in 'the ashes' of the archive" (Luiselli 2019: 23). The frenzy she feels as she negotiates the urgency of her pursuit alongside its enormity is palpable in the pacing of passages like the following one in which she describes her process:

---

echo inventory about Geronimo that is never transcribed within the novel and seems to only rarely involve interaction with Apache or Indigenous communities). The text does obliquely suggest anti-Indigeneity—the husband describes Geronimo as someone who "was Mexican by nationality but hated Mexicans . . . [because] Mexican soldiers had killed his three children, his mother, and his wife" (Luiselli 2019: 45)—but it does not substantively engage with those issues.

> I pored over reports and articles about child refugees and tried to gather infor-
> mation on what was happening beyond the New York immigration court, at the
> border, in detention centers and shelters. I got in touch with lawyers, attended
> conferences of the New York City Bar Association, had private meetings with
> non-profit workers and community organizers. I collected loose notes, scraps,
> cutouts, quotes copied down on cards, letters, maps, photographs, lists of words,
> clippings, tape-recorded testimonies. (23)

The result of this research is the curation of her bankers box, a collection of "well-
filtered material" that she hopes will help her "understand how to document the
children's crisis at the border" (24). She describes the contents of the box early
on, saying,

> I had a few photos, some legal papers, intake questionnaires used for court
> screenings, maps of migrant deaths in the southern deserts, and a folder with doz-
> ens of "Migrant Mortality Reports" printed from online search engines that locate
> the missing, which listed bodies found in those deserts, the possible cause of
> death, and their exact location. At the very top of the box, I placed a few books I'd
> read and thought would help me think about the whole project from a certain nar-
> rative distance: *The Gates of Paradise*, by Jersey Andrzejewski; *The Children's
> Crusade*, by Marcel Schwob, *Belladonna*, by Daša Drndić; *Le Goût de l'archive*,
> by Arlette Farge; and a little red book I hadn't read yet, called *Elegies for Lost
> Children*, by Ella Camposanto. (24)

The photos and papers referenced reappear later in the novel when they are
recorded in the unnumbered pages that transpose the material contents of the
woman's box, Box V. The images and transcriptions included in the unnumbered
section take the earlier references and expand on them. For example, when the
woman narrates the contents of her box, she notes that there is a folder of migrant
mortality reports. But when the box is documented as a part of the larger archival
novel, the reports are transcribed, and the reader can see the information listed
in each document. Box V also contains the photographs and loose notes both
character narrators reference and produce.

    The multiple accounts of the woman's archive loop back to other sections
of the text and contribute to the accumulative velocity and palimpsestic experience of the novel. For example, one of the authors listed in her archive is Arlette
Farge, who is quoted in the opening epigraph I cited above: "An archive presupposes an archivist, a hand that collects and classifies." Even materials that are
not explicitly referential produce echoes and reverberations through a layering
of the novel's thematic curations. Three of the books referenced are allusions to
experimental texts about children on dangerous journeys or memory and historical violence (*The Gates of Paradise*, by Jersey Andrzejewski; *The Children's
Crusade*, by Marcel Schwob; *Belladonna*, by Daša Drndić), and the final novel,

Lost Children Elegies, is a work of experimental fiction attributed to a fictional-ized author named Ella Camposanto but actually written by Luiselli. *Elegies* is a story loosely based on a mythologized children's crusade in Europe in 1212 that is reimagined into "a not-so-distant future in a region that can possibly be mapped back to North Africa, the Middle East, and southern Europe, or to Cen-tral and North America" (Luiselli 2019: 139). In a footnote at the end of the novel, Luiselli tells the reader that "*The Elegies* are composed by means of a series of allusions to literary works that are about voyaging, journeying, migrating, etc.," (many of which are included in the family's bankers boxes) like Homer's *Odys-sey*, *The Children's Crusade* by Marcel Schwob, *Pedro Páramo* by Juan Rulfo, and *Heart of Darkness* by Joseph Conrad. *Elegies* is thus, itself, "a repurpos[ing] and recombin[ation]" of rhythmic cadences, imagery, lexicon, and "words and word pairings" whose effect is to connect journeying to a descent into the under-world (380).[13]

The citations I outlined here are just a small portion of those included in the novel. There are six more bankers boxes transcribed; epigraphs that cite authors like Gloria Anzaldúa and Natalie Diaz as well as James Fenton and Virginia Woolf; folders that contain citations of scholars like Brent Hayes Edwards, Marisa Fuentes, Arjun Appadurai, and Frances Dolan; and narrative accounts of events that reference authors like William Golding, Ralph Ellison, and Jack Kerouac, photographers like Sally Mann, Emmet Gowin, Larry Clark, and Nan Goldin, and songs from Kendrick Lamar, Andrew Jackson Jihad, and Laurie Anderson. One could, of course, read without chasing the citations, but regardless of whether you choose to follow any of the references, the book immerses you in narrative patterns and layers that are difficult to ignore. Keeping track of the connections and resonances within the text is an overwhelming task, one that can produce a reading and research experience that mimics the woman narrator's. At one point, she describes her emotional response to her work on the trip, saying, "All I see in

---

13. This description is an expansion and echo of the woman narrator's description of *Elegies* earlier in the novel:

The book is written in a series of numbered fragments, sixteen in total; each fragment is called an "elegy," and each elegy is partly composed using a series of quotes. Throughout the book, these quotes are borrowed from different writers. They are either "freely translated" by the author or "recombined" to the point that some are not traceable back to their original versions. In this first English edition (published in 2014), the translator has decided to translate all bor-rowed quotes directly from the author's Italian and not from the original sources. (Luiselli 2019: 142–43)

hindsight is the chaos of history repeated, over and over, reenacted, reinterpreted, the world, its fucked-up heart palpitating underneath us, failing, messing up again and again as it winds its way around a sun. And in the middle of it all, tribes, families, people, all beautiful things falling apart, debris, dust, erasure" (Luiselli 2019: 146). The process of trying to create an archive that might explain and undermine the dominant narratives of the refugee crisis at the US-Mexico border is demoralizing. Her research demonstrates the pervasive systems of oppression that result in global migrant crises and lost children. To use the language of BAN scholarship, her archive makes visible "the huge cultural realities" that connect the US-Mexico border to the state of global society more broadly. And part of the ambition of this novel is that it demonstrates that accounting for that cultural reality, trying to archive everything from microagressions to mortalities and intimate family histories to global crises, produces a feverish response.

The term *archive fever* comes from the translation of Derrida's (1995: 12) conceptualization of *mal d'archive* as "archive fever." Derrida suggests that archival "fever" or "evil" is the result of the contradiction between a conservation and destruction drive: "There would be no archival desire without the radical finitude, without the possibility of a forgetfulness" (19). To experience the *"mal"* of the archive means "to burn with a passion . . . never to rest, interminably, from searching for the archive right before it slips away. It is to run after the archive, even if there's too much of it, right where something in it anarchives itself. It is to have a compulsive, repetitive, and nostalgic desire for the archive" (91). There has been debate about the accuracy of translating *mal d'archive* as archive fever, and Derrida's theories are more nuanced than these excerpted quotes suggest, but the tension between forgetfulness and remembrance and the description of the outcome of negotiating those irreconcilable aims is a productive one for the histories I have outlined in this essay. The feverish imagination of Luiselli's archival novel is a response to how difficult it is to create flexible, responsive structures of remembrance, to how difficult it is to make visible the systems of othering that dictate who is forgotten.

5. On Conclusions: Stories That Never End

Marco Codebó (2007: 8–9) notes that "the paginated book, in its very essence, implies sequence. It respectfully but intentionally asks readers to follow the numeric order of its pages from the first to the last"; it implies the "beginning, middle, and end" that the woman narrator describes as the format of a "proper story." *Lost Children* is a paginated text, a document with a sequence, but it is also an archival fiction that encourages recursive attention, flipping back to previous sections, hunting for the documents in each box, and following the trails of extratextual information hinted at in the allusions and references. Ostensibly, the narrative of the text concludes with a transcribed sound "document" produced by the boy, but the final section in the archive of the book is actually a works cited in which Luiselli describes the sources she has used and the novel-within-a-novel she created. In that document, she explains, "The archive that sustains this novel is both an inherent and a visible part of the central narrative. In other words, references to sources—textual, musical, visual, or audio-visual—are not meant as side notes, or ornaments that decorate the story, but function as intralinear markers that point to the many voices in the conversation that the book sustains with the past" (Luiselli 2019: 379). As a whole, the works cited argues for the importance of reading *Lost Children* in circulation with other texts. It asks us to consider tracing the citations and reverberations that the novel develops and to imagine the archival novel as a strategic response, a reflexive form that encourages an ongoing process of "shufflings" and "reorderings."

James Wood (2000) suggests that the length of BANs provokes "a soothing sense that it might never have to end, that another thousand or two thousand pages might easily be added," but in Luiselli's text that feeling of interminability is a judgment, a critique of an unending story of racial oppression to which "another thousand or two thousand pages might easily be added." In *Lost Children Archive*, the woman narrator suggests that "stories don't fix anything or save anyone" but they can "with a certain rage and fierceness" articulate "a specific pulse, a gaze, a rhythm, the right way of telling the story" that might "make the world both more complex and more tolerable" (Luiselli 2019: 185–86).

Luiselli's big, ambitious archival novel does not seek to produce a totalizing-synthetic representation that "understand[s] and represent[s]" one of "the most pressing questions of our time" (Ercolino 2014: 5, 10) because as the woman narrator explains, understanding (like mastery) "has a passive connotation" (Luiselli 2019: 174).[14] Instead, big, ambitious archival fiction is a space for "recognition,

---

14. The quote from *Tell Me* with which I began this essay suggests that "before anything can be *understood*, it has to be narrated many times," so it seems that Luiselli revises the notion of "understanding" in *Tell Me* into a more recursive process of "re-cognizing" in *Lost Children*.

in the sense of *re-cognizing*, knowing again, for a second or third time, like an echo of knowledge" (174; emphasis added).[15] Echoes are epistemological tools, and even though narrative form is contradictory, contested, and negotiated, an archival novel like this one, with its recursive, ambitious form, can highlight the absences of refugee voices, attend to the histories of violence that have led to their disappearance, and refuse to posit an answer to how the story ends if we have to keep telling it again and again.

Valentina Montero Román is an assistant professor of English at the University of California, Irvine.

Works Cited

Berwick, Isabel. 2017. "Novelist Valeria Luiselli on Nationality, Migration, and Trump." *Financial Times*, October 13.

Blackwell, Maylei. 2011. *¡Chicana Power! Contested Histories of Feminism in the Chicano Movement*. Austin: University of Texas Press.

Clark, Hilary. 1992. "Encyclopedic Discourse." *SubStance*, no. 67: 95–110.

Codebó, Marco. 2007. "The Dossier Novel: (Post)Modern Fiction and the Discourse of the Archive." *InterActions: UCLA Journal of Education and Information Studies* 3, no. 1. escholarship.org/uc/item/0289g0dx.

Derrida, Jacques. 1995. *Archive Fever: A Freudian Impression*. Translated by Eric Prenowitz. Chicago: University of Chicago Press.

Ercolino, Stefano. 2012. "The Maximalist Novel." *Comparative Literature* 64, no. 3: 241–56.

Ercolino, Stefano. 2014. *The Maximalist Novel: From Thomas Pynchon's "Gravity's Rainbow" to Roberto Bolaño's "2666."* Translated by Albert Sbragia. New York: Bloomsbury.

Foucault, Michel. 2003. "Lives of Infamous Men." In *The Essential Foucault*, edited by Paul Rabinow and Nikolas Rose, 279–93. New York: New Press.

Greif, Mark. 2009. "'The Death of the Novel' and Its Afterlives: Toward a History of the 'Big, Ambitious Novel.'" *boundary 2* 36, no. 2: 11–30.

Hartman, Saidiya. 2008. "Venus in Two Acts." *Small Axe*, no. 26: 1–14.

Hartman, Saidiya. 2020. *Wayward Lives, Beautiful Experiments: Intimate Histories of Riotous Black Girls, Troublesome Women, and Queer Radicals*. New York: Norton.

---

15. This quote is actually from a section about the woman narrator forgiving her mother for leaving their family to join the guerilla movement, but I like the idea of re-cognizing as a term for demonstrating how echoes might function as epistemological tools, and so I have adapted it here.

Herman, Luc. 2005. "Encyclopedic Novel." In *Routledge Encyclopedia of Narrative Theory*, edited by David Herman, Manfred Jahn, and Marie-Laure Ryan, 137–38. London: Routledge.

Holloway, Karla F. C. 2017. "Revision and (Re)membrance: A Theory of Literary Structures in Literature by African-American Women Writers." *African American Review* 50, no. 4: 765–79.

Lazo, Rodrigo. 2010. "Migrant Archives: New Routes in and out of American Studies." In *Teaching and Studying the Americas: Cultural Influences from Colonialism to the Present*, edited by Anthony B. Pinn, Caroline F. Levander, and Michael O. Emerson, 36–54. New York: Palgrave Macmillan.

LeClair, Tom. 1989. *The Art of Excess: Mastery in Contemporary American Fiction*. Urbana: University of Illinois Press.

Letzler, David. 2012. "The Paradox of Encyclopedic Fiction." Paper presented at the Northeast Modern Language Association conference, St. John Fisher College, Rochester, NY, March 15–18. www.academia.edu/6045215/The_Paradox_of_Encyclopedic_Fiction.

Lugones, Maria. 2010. "Toward a Decolonial Feminism." *Hypatia* 25, no. 4: 742–59.

Luiselli, Valeria. 2017. *Tell Me How It Ends: An Essay in 40 Questions*. Minneapolis: Coffee House.

Luiselli, Valeria. 2019. *Lost Children Archive*. New York: Alfred A. Knopf.

Manoff, Marlene. 2004. "Theories of the Archive from across the Disciplines." *portal: Libraries and the Academy* 4, no. 1: 9–25.

Molina, Natalia. 2014. *How Race Is Made in America: Immigration, Citizenship, and the Historical Power of Racial Scripts*. Berkeley: University of California Press.

Molina, Natalia. 2018. "Understanding Race as a Relational Concept" *Modern American History* 1, no. 1: 101–10.

Mukherjee, Bharati. 1988. "Immigrant Writing: Give Us Your Maximalists!" Sunday Book Review. *New York Times*, August 28.

"Oración del migrante / The migrant's prayer." n.d. *World Prayers*. www.worldprayers.org/archive/prayers/adorations/the_journey_towards_you_lord_is_life.html (accessed August 16, 2020).

Pérez, Emma. 1999. *The Decolonial Imaginary: Writing Chicanas into History*. Bloomington: Indiana University Press.

Sandoval, Chela. 1991. "US Third World Feminism: The Theory and Method of Oppositional Consciousness in the Postmodern World Genders." *Genders*, no. 10: 1–24.

Wood, James. 2000. "Human, All Too Inhuman." *New Republic*, July 24: 41–45.

Woolf, Virginia. 1981. *A Room of One's Own*. New York: Harcourt Brace Jovanovich.

"An Indigenous Sovereignty of the Imagination": Reenvisioning the Great Australian Novel in Alexis Wright's *Carpenteria*

LIZ SHEK-NOBLE

Alexis Wright's second novel, *Carpentaria* ([2006] 2009), received critical acclaim following its publication in 2006 by the small press Giramondo. In addition to being the 2007 recipient of Australia's foremost literary prize, the Miles Franklin Literary Award, *Carpentaria* was also awarded in the same year the Queensland Premier's Fiction Book Award, the Australian Literature Society Gold Medal, the Victorian Premier's Vance Palmer Prize for Fiction, and the ABIA Literary Fiction Book of the Year Award (Devlin-Glass 2008: 392). The astounding critical success of *Carpentaria* is in itself noteworthy but perhaps even more so is the fact that Wright was the first Indigenous author to win the Miles Franklin Award outright since its inception in 1957 (Perlez 2007: para. 3).[1] Although celebrated in its own right for its formal inventiveness and as a magic realist work "that both honours Indigenous sovereignty and culture and attests to the ravages wrought by colonisation" (Atkinson 2013: para. 1), *Carpentaria* also came at a propitious time in the history of Indigenous literary production. The Australian Bicentenary in 1988 (re)ignited public debate about the damaging legacies of British colonialism while fueling the creative output of Indigenous authors including Kim Scott, Jack Davis, and Sally Morgan (Wheeler 2013: 1–2). Moreover, collections such as *The Literature of Australia* (Jose 2009) and the *Macquarie PEN Anthology of Australian Aboriginal Literature* (Heiss and Minter 2008) served as

---

1. Kim Scott's *Benang* (1999) was the joint winner of the Miles Franklin Literary Award in 2000.

Genre, Vol. 54, No. 2   July 2021
DOI 10.1215/00166928-9263065   © 2021 by University of Oklahoma

monuments to the robust contribution made by Aboriginal authors to Australia's literary history. Additionally, such anthologies showcased the stylistic breadth of works by Indigenous authors, thereby loosening the dominant association of Aboriginal writing with autobiography and memoir to include a diverse array of genres (Polak 2017: 13).

Yet such milestones in the country's literary production also raise questions about the place of *Carpentaria* within an imagined canon of Australian literature. Iva Polak (2017) and Paul Sharrad (2009) have proclaimed *Carpentaria* as a "great Australian novel," noting that its epic scope, polyvocality, and "'classic' broad vision" (Sharrad 2009: 52) of rural life in the remote outpost of the country's tropical north satisfy the reader's yearning for a novel that captures the proverbial spirit of the nation while possessing adequate literary complexity to warrant repeated study (Buell 2014: 6).[2] Acclaimed novelist Alex Miller (Meyer 2009: paras. 2, 3) went further to label *Carpentaria* as *the* great Australian novel and Wright as "the Australian Joyce and Rabelais rolled into one." He further predicted that neither Wright nor any other Australian author would create another work that could possibly compare to *Carpentaria* in its literary significance and innovation: "It's not going to be repeated." Meanwhile, Adam Shoemaker (2008: 55) declared that *Carpentaria* is "the greatest, most inventive and most mesmerizing Indigenous epic ever produced in Australia." Shoemaker (2008: 55) further proposed that Wright's second novel will surely be regarded as "a landmark text in Australian literary history" due to its capacity to defy formal conventions. Nonetheless, I argue that the politics of *Carpentaria* work against its categorization as a/the great Australian novel by refusing comfortable narratives of national identity and unity. Set in the fictional town of Desperance in the Gulf of Carpentaria, the novel is a multigenerational epic that utilizes stories from the Dreaming to lend urgency to its denouncement of Aboriginal deaths in custody, land degradation by multinational mining corporations, and a contemporary Australia fractured along racial and intracommunity lines. Wright has been vocal about the intended readership of her novel, stating that she "didn't want a book that suited the mainstream" (Wright, quoted in Perlez 2007: para. 4). It is easy to imagine here that the "mainstream" audience to which she

---

2. While Lawrence Buell's (2014) monograph is principally interested in the historical and sociocultural conditions under which the Great American Novel (GAN) came into being, he concedes that Australia has a strong GAN tradition to rival the United States, "albeit less longstanding . . . with a shifting set of nominees and definitional traits" (11).

refers are non-Aboriginal, a point that Indigenous author and scholar Anita M. Heiss (2003: 16) makes when observing that "a general Aboriginal reading experience is yet to be fostered." Indeed, in an essay for *Heat*, Wright (2007: 89) makes reference to the difficulty that non-Indigenous readers may experience with *Carpentaria* because it was written "as though some old Aboriginal person was telling the story." For Wright, it was necessary for her to compose *Carpentaria* in a style "reminiscent . . . of oral storytelling" (80) as a means of carving out a space by which to explore the relevance of ancestral time and history to the contemporary Indigenous experience. By the same token, the orality of *Carpentaria*, which involves a blending of formal and colloquial registers, Aboriginal English and Australian English, and second- and third-person narrative voices, unsettles the assumed white Western reader and their claims to knowledge and history. For Alison Ravenscroft (2010: 214), the "radical doubleness" and "poetics of equivocality" in *Carpentaria* seek to demonstrate that Indigenous knowledge is inaccessible and unassimilable for non-Aboriginal readers: "Time and again the Law falls out of the scene of white Western imagining."

This article sets out to resituate *Carpentaria* within contemporary discussions of "big, ambitious novels" (BANs) by contemporary women novelists of color. In keeping with the contention of this special issue that BANs are mainly "the purview of men," my article considers how *Carpentaria* as a novel by an Indigenous Australian woman novelist problematizes the inherent gender and racial hierarchies involved in literary canon formation. I explore ways that *Carpentaria* simultaneously invites *and* resists its inclusion into a so-called canon of "great Australian novels." My main argument is that the experimentalism of the novel, typified in its cacophonous array of narrative voices and use of vernacular registers works against the racialized and assimilative agendas that characterize discussions of Australian nation-building. While the "great Australian novel" purportedly reflects "a common understanding of being Australian" (Elder [2020] 2007: 26; see also Polak 2017: 4) and "a fascination . . . with Australian traditions and their place in the modern world" (Dixon 2005: 254), I argue that *Carpentaria* does not aspire to inclusion in this privileged textual space precisely because this discursive site represents a white majority viewpoint that rejects Indigenous knowledge and cultural claims. The first section will provide a review of scholarship on *Carpentaria* and account for its inclusion within a set of "great Australian novels" (GANs). The section will look at critics' tendency to legitimize *Carpentaria*'s designation as a "GAN" by drawing attention to Xavier Herbert's *Cap-*

ricornia (1939) and *Poor Fellow My Country* (1975) as its literary predecessors. It will also comment on the influence of magic realism on *Carpentaria*. Then, I will conduct a close analysis of key moments in the novel wherein Aboriginal and Western epistemologies and cosmologies come into contact. Contrary to scholars (Molloy 2012; Devlin-Glass 2008) who read a politics of Indigenous reconciliation *or* separatism in the novel, I argue that Wright's vision of a future Australia can neither be sustained through total rejection nor harmonization with white settler culture. *Carpentaria* imagines Indigenous sovereignty as surviving, and more importantly, thriving through its persistent engagement with contradictory epistemological, cosmological, and ideological frameworks. Such contact gives voice to tension and antagonism rather than reconciliation. Using Homi Bhabha's ([1994] 2004) notion of the third space, I view the orality of *Carpentaria*, in which Wright found a way to "embody both the negative effects of colonialism and her proud Aboriginal heritage" (Atkinson 2013: para. 3) as representative of a transcultural logic that "articulate[s] antagonistic and oppositional elements without the redemptive rationality of sublation or transcendence" (Bhabha [1994] 2004: 38).

Carpentaria and/as the "Great Australian Novel"

Reflecting on the tenth anniversary of *Carpentaria*'s publication in an article in the *Guardian*, Wright (2017: para. 14) described her novel as "this strange blackfella book in the time of John Howard." Embedded in this remark is a series of assumptions about the novel's intended readership, its wider reception among (non-Indigenous) Australians during the conservative and paternalistic Howard government, and its overall value within the field of Australian literature as a whole. To appreciate Wright's comment entirely, it is necessary to make reference to a noted irony in the history of *Carpentaria*'s critical reception. On the day Wright was awarded the Miles Franklin Literary Award, the Howard government announced the Northern Territory National Emergency Response (colloquially known as "the Intervention"). The Intervention established a task force to deal with claims of rampant sexual abuse of minors in Aboriginal communities in the wake of the "Little Children Are Sacred" Report. Prominent Indigenous leaders did not universally accept the Intervention as an appropriate response to the crisis; as Shoemaker (2008: 56) notes, the failure to assign any Aboriginal people as part of the police and military task force demonstrated the federal government's persistent failure to recognize the expertise of its Elders in dealing with intracommunity problems. A related concern was that the Racial Discrimination Act of 1975 was suspended in order to implement various measures of the Intervention, including the management of Indigenous people's incomes and bans on gambling, alcohol, and pornography. The suspension of this Act threatened the basic human rights of Indigenous Australians, allowing the government to "seize control of many aspects of the daily lives of residents in 73 targeted remote communities" (Perche 2017: para. 2). Diana Perche (2017: para. 21) goes further to explain how the Intervention constituted a decisive break in the federal government's existing "approach of supporting Indigenous self-determination," leading to the introduction of "a new paternalism, or guardianship, where 'government knows best' and Indigenous difference is understood as a negative, or a deficit which must be reformed."

Returning to Wright's (2017) earlier comment, the author draws a political separation between white and Indigenous Australians and thereby suggests that *Carpentaria* will have limited appeal for non-Indigenous readers. Additionally, in identifying her book as "strange," Wright confers a "minor" status to *Carpentaria* because of its potential esoterism and inability to sit comfortably within established rules of (Western) fiction. And finally, to underscore her intention to write a novel for a specific audience, Wright identifies *Carpentaria* as a "blackfella book." This exclusionary project—that is, to write a novel about Aboriginal Australians *for* Aboriginal people—is not unique to *Carpentaria*. In an essay published after her first novel, *Plains of Promise*, Wright (2002: 19) unapologetically states, "I do not think of other people as readers of my book outside of my own community." Wright is referring to those who are part of her immediate Waanyi community, as well as the wider pan-Aboriginal nation set apart from the white, Western majority of Australia. Elsewhere in her essay, Wright (2002: 13) clearly states that mainstream Western readers are uninterested in learning about "the living hell of many Aboriginal people," instead preferring to shy away from the struggle that they face in order to survive in contemporary Australia: "We [Indigenous Australians] sit in hospitals watching our cultural knowledge sliding away from us, which the rest of Australia are glad to see buried, while they hurry to the beach with their lighthearted reading, about similar lives to themselves" (Wright 2002: 18).

What accounts, then, for the critical *and* mainstream popularity[3] of *Carpentaria* in light of Wright's firm belief that general Western audiences would derive little narrative, thematic, and political interest from the novel? To answer this question, we need to consider further what has made critics like the Indigenous author Tara June Winch (2020: para. 10) call Wright "our country's great literary voice" and others like Polak (2017: 14) state confidently that *Carpentaria* "certainly belong[s] to the story of the 'Great Australian Novel.'" My argument is that there are three primary maneuvers critics use to justify the placement of *Carpentaria* within a privileged set of GANs. The first is to situate *Carpentaria* within the literary genre of magic realism or to trace its lineage back to Herbert's *Capricornia*. The second way that critics account for the "greatness" of *Carpentaria* is through reference to its historical maximality. As Buell (2014: 29) contends, "a GAN cannot be tiny." As a novel that brings "the ancestral realm into a story of all times" (Wright 2017: para. 1) by depicting foundational aspects of the Dreaming, including the formation of land and rivers by the Ancestral Serpent, *Carpentaria* is a saga encompassing the whole of Indigenous history. The final tendency is for critics to celebrate the formal innovations of *Carpentaria*, where its "rapid shifts in mood and tone, its contractions of and jumps in time, and its conscious stylistic idiosyncrasies . . . [make it,] to borrow a phrase from the narrator, a novel 'on a grand scale of course'" (Lowry 2008: para. 14).

Wright on Magic Realism, Critics on *Capricornia*

A review of scholarship on *Carpentaria* reveals two main ways that critics seek to legitimize the novel as a candidate for GAN status. The first way is to identify how *Carpentaria* recalls "classic" Australian novels in either its setting or literary style. In his review of the novel, Ian Syson (2007: 85) notes that his experience of reading *Carpentaria* recalled his "sense of satisfaction" in having completed Patrick White's *The Tree of Man* (1955). Syson (2007: 85) draws this comparison not only based on the sheer size of the novels but also their similar end result for the reader; both of them exist as a powerful record "of our time," whose relevance extends beyond the singular lives of its characters to encompass a defining spirit of the Australian nation. In this way, *Carpentaria* and *The Tree of Man* appear

---

3. Jane Perlez (2007) notes that by 2007 *Carpentaria* had already sold twenty-five thousand copies and was in its sixth printing.

to encapsulate a defining quality of GANs, which is their ability to shift between micro and macro levels in their exploration of themes germane to national identity: belonging, historical traditions, and community. As Robert Dixon (2005: 254–55) remarks, the "Great Australian Novel must be grounded in a regional or local identity, while also attaining more national or universal significance." Nevertheless, Syson's reference to White is a rarity in scholarship pertaining to *Carpentaria*, for the most common predecessor mentioned is Xavier Herbert. Elizabeth Lowry (2008) espies a family resemblance between *Carpentaria* and Herbert's sweeping historical epic, *Capricornia* (1938). Like *Carpentaria*, Herbert's novel is set in a fictional location named "Capricornia" that is bedeviled by long-standing and bloody conflict between white settlers and the Indigenous people of the area,[4] offering a "fictional account of the clash of cultures from which contemporary Australian society developed" (Lowry 2008). Similarly, Chris Gibson, Susan Luckman, and Julie Willoughby-Smith (2010: 32) identify a "lineage of exploration of the [Australian] frontier experience" in *Carpentaria* and *Capricornia*. Implicit in these associations is a romanticized vision of the frontier as a place that draws in ragtag characters with its promises of adventure and improved fortunes. Elsewhere, Frances Devlin-Glass (2008) and Liz Conor and Ann McGrath (2017) attribute thematic and formal credit to Herbert by way of *Poor Fellow My Country*. Devlin-Glass (2008: 82) argues, "Like Herbert's underrated work . . . its [*Carpentaria*'s] key concerns seem to be to mobilize Aboriginal sacred knowledge for political purposes." The transnational mining exploits of Gurfurritt in *Carpentaria* are for Devlin-Glass (2008) a powerful instrument of neocolonial oppression, and it is only through the deployment of the Aboriginal Dreaming that a relationship of reciprocity between humans and the natural environment can emerge. On the other hand, Conor and McGrath (2017) observe that in both *Poor Fellow My Country* and *Carpentaria*, the land is registered as an active agent on par with its human characters. By elevating the land to the status of a character (Wright 2004: 121), Conor and McGrath (2017: 64) argue that Wright critiques the "shallowness" of European time against the expansive and "deep" time of Indigenous culture.

---

4. Paul Sharrad (2009: 57) observes further family resemblances between *Capricornia* and *Carpentaria* "apart from the similarity of its title, length and northern setting." Sharrad mentions that *Carpentaria* is "a sprawling narrative of character sketches, satiric denunciations of careless and brutish white life in the tropics and its accompanying racism, and a vision of a land in which life generally is both cheap and largely absurd under the random impact of 'cockeyed bob' whirlwinds, torrential downpours, and what Thomas Hardy called 'life's little ironies' of haphazard circumstance."

In their tendency to draw a line of influence from Herbert and White to Wright, I find that critics are attempting to confer prestige onto *Carpentaria* and ease its transition into a venerated and finite collection of GANs. Yet I cannot also dismiss that such a move is also an incorporative strategy that risks effacing the gender and racial dynamics that influence the selection of some works as part of a discursive literary center while relegating others to the periphery. As a woman Aboriginal writer, Wright's inclusion in a so-called list of GANs by way of white Australian men authors like Herbert and White can be viewed as an attempt to domesticate and reclaim *Carpentaria* as a product of coloniality, rather than its antithesis. Moreover, celebration of Wright's novel can also be interpreted as a calculated act to legitimize writing by Aboriginal authors that adhere to Western standards of what "good writing" *should* entail, including literary referentiality, formal experimentation, and narrative complexity. My comments here bear similarity to Ravenscroft's (2010) criticism of scholarship linking *Carpentaria* and Wright with *Capricornia* and Herbert. Ravenscroft (2010: 195) finds that such moves "refuse the text's unfamiliarity, its strangeness to a white reader." She also notes that critics' eagerness to submerge the strangeness of *Carpentaria* under a magic realist model inadvertently repeats the cultural hierarchies that the novel seeks to undo by associating "Indigeneity with magic, irrationality, delusion and dream, and whiteness with realism, reality and rationality" (Ravenscroft 2010: 197).

Justine Seran (2013: 4) shares Ravenscroft's concern; she contends that in placing elements of Indigenous cosmology under the framework of magic realism, critics strip these elements of their contextual and semantic specificity in the Dreaming. Notwithstanding Ravenscroft's (2010) and Seran's (2013) reservations, there is justification for making connections between the representation of Indigenous cosmology and magic realism in Wright's novel. This justification comes from Wright herself, who in numerous essays and interviews has repeatedly mentioned she drew inspiration from magic realist authors when writing *Carpentaria*. For her, Carlos Fuentes, Gabriel García Márquez, and Patrick Chamoiseau are able to capture the sense of "all times" in their novels that closely approximates the expression of the Dreaming through oral performance. Wright finds that these authors show the present as a concatenation of moments stretching back to ancestral time. In particular, Wright (2007: 216) credits Chamoiseau for "show[ing] me how to write all times." This technique of temporal accretion was critical to Wright's project in conveying the rich history of Indigenous Australia, as a way to show the various sagas that its people have been a part of for thousands of years: "Today, we have sagas in our lives with our relationship with the rest of the country that have taken the last 200 odd years. That's another saga that has been attached to the old traditional sagas" (Wright 2004: 121).[5]

Critical scholarship on *Carpentaria* attributes the panoply of spirits in *Carpentaria* and the interruption of the spiritual world into physical reality to a magic realist influence. The popularity of magic realism as a genre in Australian fiction from the 1990s and beyond deserves mention here as reflecting a shift in GAN discussion following the Australian bicentennial. For Dixon (2005: 254), the bicentennial had a profound influence on the arts, leading to the belief that the GAN must reflect a transnational shift in the literary marketplace through exploring Australian identity on regional, national, and international levels. Using Tim Winton's *Cloudstreet* (1991) as his example, Dixon (2005: 257) notes that stylistically the novel can "at once be read back into the Australian tradition and forward into certain forms of internationalism." The internationalism of which Dixon (2005: 257) speaks is its connections with magic realism, most notably Gabriel García Márquez's *One Hundred Years of Solitude* in its interweaving of historical saga with myth. Critics' evaluations of *Carpentaria* as a novel influenced by magic realism demonstrate attention toward intradiegetic shifts between the real and the mythic, along with the transnational entanglements of the literary marketplace. Syson (2007: 85) locates homegrown precursors for *Carpentaria* in the works of Peter Carey and Richard Flanagan but finds Wright's novel is "a major Australian landmark in that genre" by adapting its magic for "more indigenous *and* Indigenous sources." Meanwhile, Devlin-Glass (2008: 392) argues *Carpentaria* adapts the genre of magic realism to include knowledge and beings from the Aboriginal Dreaming to apply pressure to the opposition of what is "real" and "problematically termed 'magic.'" For Devlin-Glass (2008: 395), the blending of the mundane and the real undoes the dynamic between the colonizing power and the colonized, which saw the rejection of Indigenous knowledge and its accompanying narratives as holding little truth value against the rigorous, "scientific" knowledge of the West. Ben Holgate (2015) also holds a similar point of view in his analysis of both *Carpentaria* and Wright's most recent novel, *The Swan Book* (2013).[6]

---

5. Wright (1998) intends to show in *Carpentaria*, as with her earlier *Plains of Promise* (1997), that Aboriginal stories and traditions far exceed "our 200 year relationship with Australian governments and the state of cross-cultural relationships here today."

6. References to magic realism appear elsewhere in scholarship by Jane Gleeson-White (2013), Anne Brewster (2010), and Diane Molloy (2012).

Certainly, there are various moments in *Carpentaria*[7] wherein the boundaries separating the material and spiritual worlds are collapsed in a way akin to magic realism. Wright underplays the extraordinariness of these occurrences to convey that neither Indigenous ontology nor epistemology can be defined according to a logic of binaries. This viewpoint directly supports Wright's (2007: 94, 81) aim in creating an "Indigenous sovereignty of the imagination," wherein Aboriginal notions of time and law could be set free from the "Australian tradition of creating boundaries and fences." To imagine Aboriginal characters and history *outside* of the borders of forced colonization required Wright to undo the association of Indigenous culture with primitivism and irrationality. In one such instance, the narrator downgrades the technological progress of the West by blithely commenting that Aboriginal people possessed the capacity for flight long before the "white man invented aeroplanes" (*C*: 195): "*You will see Aboriginal people flying around themselves*" (*C*: 195). To lend further veracity to the belief that the Indigenous world does not observe strict borders between the empirical and the spiritual, the narrator turns to Will Phantom's scar to show the continued relevance of ancestral history to the present moment: "They said Will's scar came from such a battle that took place in the skies with sea eagle spirits over the Gulf sea, long before he was born" (*C*: 195). Other representative examples of Wright having adapted elements of magic realism for an Indigenous cosmology and purpose include Norm's quest to bury Elias in an underwater grove belonging to groupers. Norm awakens from a dream in which he explores their glittering, jewellike world. The groupers perform a dance that culminates in their ascension into the sky along with Elias's spirit:

> Awoken by the scuttering and scurrying of small creatures escaping with his dreams, he looked over the water and saw the big tank fish—gropers swimming together in congregations of fifty or more like dark clouds arriving from the distance. . . . Norm wiped their salty spray from his face, as he studied them swimming through the ocean of air, to ascend into the sky world of the Milky Way. . . . Norm, drifting in and out of sleep, caught a glimpse of the fish become stars shooting back in the skies, and finally, the night caravan moving further and further away on its journey. He knew at once Elias was up there with them. (*C*: 246–47)

In a half-awake and half-dreaming state, Norm watches reverently as the gropers ascend into the sky and morph into stars. Here, the groupers bridge the

---

7. All subsequent citations for Wright's *Carpentaria* ([2006] 2009) will appear in the central text as *C*.

distance between sea and sky, for they not only swim "through the ocean of air" but transform into stars on their arrival "into the sky world of the Milky Way." With this, Wright demonstrates the intersubstantiation of all elements in the Indigenous sacred, along with its capacity to harbor foreignness and contradiction in its (porous) limits. The passage also suggests the powerful alignment of Indigenous peoples with totemic spirits. Throughout the novel, Norm Phantom is repeatedly associated with the sea and its inhabitants; he is not only a skilled boater but also possesses a remarkable gift for taxidermy, transforming rotting and dull-scaled fish into glittering treasures. With the return of Elias's body to the Grouper dreaming place, Norm reaches a greater understanding of the interconnectedness of human and animal ecologies. Devlin-Glass (2008: 404) finds that Elias's burial in this place "lyrically depicts" the "plenum metaphysic," that is, an ontology where nonhuman animals are seen as "'other selves' and kin," such that Elias's death is a renewal of, rather than end to, his being.

A Saga Spanning "All Times"

According to Ken Stewart (1983: 41), a key characteristic of GANs is to present a "dualistic frame of reference" that combines the specificity of present events with the broad strokes of the historical epic. *Carpentaria* fulfills this characteristic but does so from an Indigenous point of view in which time is "ancient, mythical, historical, and contemporary at once" (Renes 2019: 56). Wright's (2007: 84) "spinning multi-stranded helix of stories" includes but is not limited to engaging with contemporary problems faced by disenfranchised Indigenous groups, such as institutional racism, the denial of native title, and their continued relegation to the literal and symbolic margins of Australian society. Instead, the novel suffuses "the new stories of our times" (Wright 2007: 80) with the epic stories of the Indigenous sacred. One such example can be found in the updated "Walkabout" performed by Mozzie Fishman and his band of followers through the desert. While this Indigenous rite of passage is typically ventured on foot, Mozzie and his crew perform the same route as their ancestors via "a long line of battered old cars heavily coated in the red-earth dust of the dry country" (*C*: 114). But perhaps the best representation of *Carpentaria*'s ability to stretch its narrative from the present all the way back to ancestral time is in the origin story from chapter 1 ("From Time Immemorial"). Here, the narrator describes the Ancestral Serpent's topographical movements in the Gulf Country, along with the deep, foundational

power that it possesses and which allows it to withstand the ecological devasta-
tions wrought upon the land by white colonialists:

> Picture the creative serpent, scoring deep into—scouring down through—the
> slippery underground of the mudflats, leaving in its wake the thunder of tunnels
> collapsing to form deep sunken valleys. The sea water following in the serpent's
> wake, swarming in a frenzy of tidal waves, soon changed colour from ocean blue
> to the yellow of mud. The water filled the swirling tracks to form the mighty
> bending rivers spread across the vast plains of the Gulf country. . . . When it fin-
> ished creating the many rivers in its wake, it created one last river, no larger or
> smaller than the others. . . . This is where the giant serpent continues to live deep
> down under the ground. . . . They say its being is porous; it permeates everything.
> It is all around in the atmosphere and is attached to the lives of the river people
> like skin. (C: 1–2)

This is perhaps Wright's most evocative description of an Indigenous temporality
at work in the novel. Ancestral time is as immediate and tangible as the atmosphere surrounding all living things; it cannot be separated from an Aboriginal
sense of belonging because it is "attached to the lives of the river people like
skin" (C: 2). This sense of the interconnectedness of Aboriginal identity with the
Dreaming recalls Bill Ashcroft, Gareth Griffiths, and Helen Tiffin's ([1989] 2002:
142) comment on what they call the "subversive capacity in Australian Aboriginal
writers" to reject the imperial authority through their "unique conception of textuality." The land is the original "text" upon which the Dreaming is written, such
that Aboriginal art and performance are always a reenactment of mythic time as it
is experienced by the individual (Ashcroft, Griffiths, and Tiffin [1989] 2002: 142).

Moreover, the narrator's comment that the Ancestral Serpent still resides
deep within its subterranean lair is a powerful reminder of the durability of
Aboriginal knowledge in spite of persistent attempts by white colonizers to erase
it from the historical record. Shortly after this passage, the narrator calls attention to the transmission of Indigenous law through oral tradition, noting that it
has been "handed down through the ages since time began" (C: 3). Wright privileges the stability of oral knowledge against what she perceives as the flimsiness
or unreliability of written information. This effectively overturns the Western
denigration of speech in favor of writing, where the former has been perceived
by colonizers as proof of the intellectual inferiority and illiteracy of Aboriginal
groups. *Carpentaria* contrasts the deep, ancestral connections of the Westside
mob with that of the Uptown folk. Norm Phantom is one such Aboriginal Elder
who "kept a library chock-a-block full of stories of the old country" in his head
(C: 235). This is in contrast to the "shallow" history of the white settlers, which
was "just a half-flick of the switch of truth—simply a memory no greater than

two lifespans" (*C*: 56). Indeed, Wright presents white settler history as being simply inferior to the sheer volume of ancestral knowledge that is contained within the minds of Aboriginal Elders and transmitted with incredible accuracy to future generations. Wright further emphasizes the fallibility of the written word in *Carpentaria* when it is discovered that Uptown's records have been "chewed by defecating vermin" and its accompanying family histories lay "in volumes wasting away in dozens of dusty cardboard boxes." Geoff Rodoreda (2017: 1) finds that in such moments Wright succeeds in privileging not only orality's connection with ancestral knowledge but also its primacy over written texts; whereas memory and oral transmission are indestructible, Western written forms are deficient and unreliable. The narrator also shows that overreliance on the written word can lead to devastating situations in which one may question their ability to separate fact from fiction. Horrified to find that Tristrum and Luke Fishman, and Aaron Ho Kum have been hanged in their cells, police officer Truthful E'Strange begins to second-guess whether he had checked on the boys before ending his nighttime shift (*C*: 343–44). He turns to his records for verification, only to introduce further doubt when his memory does not match up with what he reads. In spite of what is written on the page, Truthful "doubted himself" and resists the urge to think he falsified the records (*C*: 344). Unlike the hapless Truthful, Mozzie Fishman needs no help to retain and transmit vital information to Will as he attempts to evade capture for sabotaging the Gurfurritt pipeline. As the narrator explains, Mozzie could give "a blow-by-blow description sung in song, unravelling a map to a Dreaming place he had never seen" (*C*: 360) but which is the ancestral home of his clan.

Formal Innovation in *Carpentaria*

In the previous section, I discussed the importance of orality in communicating the expansive sagas and history of the Indigenous Dreaming. The formal inventiveness of *Carpentaria*, of which orality is a part, deserves special attention as it is another criterion used by critics to justify the placement of the novel within a tradition of GANs. In her laudatory review of the novel, Atkinson (2013: paras. 3, 21) claims that the "experimental, allegorical, sometimes humorous and often startlingly lyrical" prose of the novel is what is bound to make *Carpentaria* "an instant classic of Australian literature." Meanwhile, Carole Ferrier (2006: 21) observes that *Carpentaria* "is a very big novel both in its size and in its qualities," the latter most notable in its ability to combine humor, irony, poetry, and myth to a heteroglossic novel "that has great confidence and authority." In this section, I would like to focus on how *Carpentaria*'s orality gives voice to its reputation as an experimental novel that cuts across various registers. Rodoreda (2017: 6) contends that Wright imbues her novel with "narratorial simulations" of interjection, exasperation, excitement, and affirmation to mirror the intimacy and suspense of oral performance. Additionally, Wright accommodates the idiosyncrasies of oral speech in *Carpentaria* through the use of malapropisms ("flown the coup" [*C*: 146]), catachresis ("gasp one single image" [*C*: 411]; "her eyes fumed" [*C*: 431]), and pronunciation mistakes (*"higgily-piggerly"* [*C*: 53]; *"just deserts"* [*C*: 150]). There are also Aboriginal words in *Carpentaria* that the narrator declines to translate, such as when Norm's boat risks being dragged out to sea by a vicious cyclone ("he saw the bad *bari* waters creeping along the side of the boat" [*C*: 289]) and when a group of Aboriginal Elders come to witness the renaming of a river in Desperance after Norm Phantom: "Traditional people gathered up for the event mumbled, *Ngabarn, Ngabarn, Mandagi*" (*C*: 9). Finally, Wright's bravura performance is evident in the way the novel jumps between different narrative voices and registers. For instance, the narrator takes on the excitable demeanor of the townsfolk upon Elias's mysterious arrival in Desperance (*C*: 71), while later shifts to second-person voice as the Gurfurritt Mine explodes, as if in cahoots with Mozzie's plot: "The soundwaves coming off the explosion in the aeroplane hangars at the biggest mine of its type in the world, Gurfurritt, were just about as tremendous a sound you could ever expect to hear on this earth. Like guyfork night. Boom! Boom! . . . We were thinking, those of us lying on the ground up in the hills smelling ash—what if our ears exploded?" (*C*: 393). The narrator's excitement is unmissable in this passage, conjuring a spectacle unparalleled in its pyrotechnics and noise. It's "like guyfork night," evoking the fireworks of another infamous plot to undermine British imperialism and the enormity of property damage in the onomatopoeic "Boom! Boom!" It is *Carpentaria*'s capacity to jump between narrative voices that shows Wright's deftness in bringing the reader into her novelistic world. Yet such shifts also deny certain readers access to complete knowledge and understanding of the Indigenous world. Rodoreda argues that the two epigraphs of *Carpentaria* that begin chapters 1 and 2 create a double framework that permits white Western readers some, but not all, access to the succeeding narrative. The first epigraph is rendered typographically distinct from the main text through its persistent capitalization:

A NATION CHANTS, *BUT WE KNOW YOUR STORY ALREADY.* THE BELLS
PEAL EVERYWHERE. CHURCH BELLS CALLING THE FAITHFUL TO
THE TABERNACLE WHERE THE GATES OF HEAVEN WILL OPEN, BUT
NOT FOR THE WICKED. CALLING INNOCENT LITTLE BLACK GIRLS
FROM A DISTANT COMMUNITY WHERE A WHITE DOVE BEARING
AN OLIVE BRANCH NEVER LANDS. LITTLE GIRLS WHO COME BACK
HOME AFTER CHURCH ON SUNDAY, WHO LOOK AROUND THEM-
SELVES AT THE HUMAN FALLOUT AND ANNOUNCE MATTER-OF-
FACTLY, *ARMAGEDDON BEGINS HERE.* (C: 1)

And so, *Carpentaria* commences with this ominous description of white Western invasion, leading to other devastating policies including those that separated
Aboriginal children from their families and communities. With this epigraph,
Rodoreda argues that Wright establishes an omniscient Aboriginal narrator who
addresses a white Western reader. The narrator dismisses the non-Aboriginal
narratee's eagerness to repeat the nation's chant: *"WE KNOW YOUR STORY
ALREADY."* Instead, the narrator introduces an alternative account of the country's colonial history, where the arrival of the First Fleet foreshadowed the end
of Aboriginal civilization as it had been previously known: *"ARMAGEDDON
BEGINS HERE."* However, I find that the narrative positionality of the epigraph
is more complicated than this. *Carpentaria*'s heterodiegetic narration is what
often confounds "a white reader's easy knowing" of the text (Ravenscroft 2010:
205) and what leads critics like Syson (2007: 86) to believe that the novel "is
frankly just too difficult to be read by non-professional or non-literary readers."
Yet this uncomfortable reading experience, emblematized in the novel's epigraph,
is also why *Carpentaria* resists simple incorporation into a white Australian literary canon (Ravenscroft 2010: 205). This resistance is evident in the ambiguity
of the first sentence: "A NATION CHANTS, *BUT WE KNOW YOUR STORY
ALREADY."* The second clause may be attributed to the voice of the Aboriginal
narrator, as per Rodoreda's (2017) analysis; yet it could also be considered as a
voice *separate* to the first narrator and instead be seen as a riposte made by a non-
Aboriginal narrator to dismiss Indigenous claims to law and sovereignty. This
internal contradiction, in which Aboriginal and Western epistemologies clash, is
what constantly unsettles the Western reader's ability to incorporate its knowledge within a framework of national unity and belonging. In the second section of
this article, I will turn to the work of Bhabha and his notion of the third space to
argue that *Carpentaria* utilizes moments of cultural syncretism *and* antagonism
to celebrate Indigenous knowledge without allowing its total incorporation into a
politics of reconciliation and renewal.

Carpentaria and the Third Space

Bhabha's third space is notorious for being one of his most nebulous, difficult, and well-known concepts, as well as one that the postcolonial scholar has spent little time explaining in his oeuvre. Apart from a select number of pages in *The Location of Culture* (2004), a preface to a collection of essays dedicated to this concept (Bhabha 2009), and an interview with Jonathan Rutherford (1990), Bhabha has yet to provide a comprehensive explanation of the third space. Robert J. C. Young (2009: 81) remarks on this curiosity, in which the concept is one of the most "widely invoked" and least understood of Bhabha's theories. Yet it is precisely the vagueness of the third space that has led to its application across a variety of fields (Ikas and Wagner 2009b: 2). In particular, the third space has become a powerful explanatory term within postcolonial studies to describe a new dialogical site that emerges through negotiation between colonial and Indigenous cultures. The third space is the hybrid outcome of the intersection of these two cultures and is therefore "new, *neither the one nor the other*" (Bhabha [1994] 2004: 37). It is important to note that the production of the third space does not lead to a synthesizing logic in which elements opposed within the colonial and Indigenous cultures are resolved. What remains as part of the third space is an oppositional, antagonistic, and differential force produced in the merging—but not dissolution—of the two cultures.

Bhabha's third space is relevant to my examination of *Carpentaria* because its logic resists a utopianism in which Indigenous culture may return to a "pure" and "original" state through the removal of white colonial culture. In this way, I argue against critics like Nonie Sharp (2007) who interpret the cyclone that destroys Desperance as a leveling force that returns the land to its rightful Indigenous owners. According to Pat Dudgeon and John Fielder (2006), Bhabha's third space challenges not only the sublation of oppositional cultures through the introduction of a reconciliatory space but also the possibility for cultures to remain static upon their contact with one another. Dudgeon and Fielder (2006: 40) argue that the third space "break[s] the simplistic logic where the dominant group tends to justify its ascendancy and the minority group uses liberationist and utopian rhetoric to construct itself as pure, innocent." The reason for Bhabha's refusal to accept a simple hierarchical inversion of colonial and Indigenous powers resides in his view that cultures are characterized by an inherent "spirit of alterity of otherness" (Bhabha, quoted in Rutherford 1990: 209). This means that transformation, rather than stability or destruction, occurs when elements from two cultural systems meet. Bhabha writes in *The Location of Culture*:

> It is only when we understand that all cultural statements and systems are con-
> structed in this contradictory and ambivalent space of enunciation, that we begin
> to understand why hierarchical claims to the inherent originality or "purity" of
> cultures are untenable. . . . It is that Third Space, though unrepresentable in itself,
> which constitutes the discursive conditions of enunciation that ensure that the
> meaning and symbols of culture have no primordial unity or fixity; that even the
> same signs can be appropriated, translated, rehistoricized and read anew. (Bhabha
> [1994] 2004: 54–55)

Returning to *Carpentaria*, I argue that its politics closely resembles the logic of the third space as both "a space of resistance as well as a space of sharing" (Ash-croft 2009: 116) between white settler and Indigenous cultures. Wright's novel entertains neither the utopian possibility of a contemporary Indigenous Australia freed from its colonial past, nor a politics of reconciliation in which a new under-standing of the nation emerges through a shared sense of belonging between the narrator and reader. As described previously, Wright's comments about the novel's intended readership, along with a narrative strategy that appears to allow some—but not total—access to Indigenous knowledge for Western readers dem-onstrate a politics that involves both antagonism and syncretism across colonial and Aboriginal cultures. Ultimately, it is this instability in both the reading of *Carpentaria* and its subject matter that I find makes it a novel that resists, rather than invites, its literary canonization. I turn now to key moments in *Carpentaria* that exemplify the oppositional and syncretic work of the third space.

Carpentaria shows the mutual transformations that occur both for colonial and Indigenous cultures as they negotiate with one another in the third space. The manner in which Angel Day appropriates objects discarded by the Uptown inhabitants attests not only to the protean nature underlying all systems but also the emergence of a new, hybrid space that is simultaneously familiar and foreign in its cultural signposts. Prior to when Angel leaves Norm for Mozzie Fishman, they live together in the Pricklebush across from the town dump. Much to her neighbors' disgust, Angel diligently sifts through the trash in the dump as a way to increase her and her family's fortunes. Ironically, Angel's fossicking is used to endorse interventionist government policies to tackle the "problem" of Indig-enous underemployment and poverty. Rather than showing her resourcefulness as a necessary strategy to survive in the Pricklebush with limited resources and support, Angel's dumpster dives are proof that the "Aboriginal plan" was working: "Bureaucratic people for the *Aborigines* department said she had 'Go.' She became a prime example of government policies at work and to prove it, they came and took pictures of her with a Pentax camera for a report" (*C*: 16). Lowry (2008: para. 9) views the "resplendently trashy" Angel as Wright's "refusal to sentimentalise her subject matter" by portraying an Aboriginal person who uses her own resources and wiliness to reject the economic and social disenfranchisement that accompanies the dispossession of her land by Uptown folk. The narrator describes Angel as a "queen" presiding over her "rubbish dump palace" (*C*: 17), a topsy-turvy characterization in which Angel is as outrageous as she is resourceful. In this way, Wright successfully expands the limiting character scripts destined for Aboriginal people in Australian fiction "as pathetic welfare cases unable to take care of ourselves, and at worst, as villainous rip-off merchants" (Wright 2007: 85). Yet the manner in which Angel appropriates certain cultural objects, particularly a statue of the Virgin Mary, is emblematic of a larger ideological contest waged between white settler and Indigenous populations since British colonization. Angel initially takes the statue from the dump, believing in its divine capacity to change her fortunes should she worship it and the Christian faith (*C*: 22–23). Yet in repainting the old and chipped statue, Angel commits an act that is both sacrilegious and culturally appropriative; her seagull "sentinels" in the dump augur her inversion of the sacred and profane in their mocking performance of a Christian hymn (*C*: 23). Once Angel returns to her home, she paints the statue "in the colour of her own likeness" (*C*: 36). The updated statue is neither reducible to the divine maternal figure of the Christian Church nor a spirit woman from the Indigenous cosmology, the latter of which is apparent later in the novel through reference to the "devil woman" *Gardajala* and the sea woman who causes Norm to become shipwrecked (*C*: 262–64). Instead, with this "Aboriginal Virgin Mary," Wright "symbolises the clash of mutually-exclusive paradigms of knowledge, 'condemned' to get on with one another" in order to forge a possible Indigenous future that is "inclusive of, but not assimilable to, the West" (Renes 2019: 53). Angel's appropriation of the statue demonstrates Bhabha's belief in the inherent instability of all signs, where even though signs we perceive as having a "primordial unity of fixity" are "appropriated, translated, rehistoricized and read anew" (2004: 55). The negotiation of this cultural artifact, in which Christian and Indigenous belief systems come into contact, results in the production of new meaning; the Virgin Mary becomes a figure dedicated to watching over and protecting "the claypan people in the Gulf country" despite outrage from

Uptown's white inhabitants over "this spectacle of irreverence for their religion" (C: 37, 38).

In Laura Joseph's (2009: 6) reading of *Carpentaria*, she asserts that the novel engages in a "politics of fantasy" that prioritizes regional knowledge over the grand narratives of nationalism and internationalism that play out in ecological discussions about Australia. Joseph finds that the geographic modifications made to the Gulf because of the cyclone challenge "the continence of 'one Australia' on the level of spatiality." As a result, *Carpentaria* offers a strong counterargument against the logic of a singular, coherent narrative of Australia in favor of Indigenous knowledge that is deeply rooted in local and regional signposts. While Joseph does not explicitly state that "the continence of 'one Australia'" is the story of the nation as told through an imperialist lens, it is not an interpretive stretch to believe Joseph has this in mind when she refers to the epigraph of *Carpentaria* as a dismissal of narratives that celebrate the colonization of Australia as the proverbial birth, rather than demise, of the country ("*ARMAGEDDON BEGINS HERE*"). Consequently, one might conclude that Desperance's destruction at the hands of "the great creators of the natural world" (C: 473) is a powerful decolonizing strategy that clears the Gulf country of all remnants of settler culture. However, rather than reinstating Indigenous sovereignty divorced from the memory (and legacy) of colonization, I find that the trash island embodies a third space where Indigenous ecology fuses with the architectural and technological monuments of Western modernity. In this respect, my analysis is reminiscent of Demelza Hall's (2012: 12) finding that, as an "uncertain bridging space," the trash island is a heterotopia. Drawing on Michel Foucault's essay, "Of Other Spaces," Hall (2012: 13) argues that the trash island functions as a heterotopia in provoking new ways by which to reimagine notions of home, belonging, and nation. However, while Foucault's heterotopias are ambivalent and in-between insofar as they refuse a simple utopian or dystopian relation to "real" time and topographies, I find that Bhabha's third space is more fruitful to my argument that the novel works against a reconciliatory gesture in which the disruption of present white Western history can lead to new formations of belonging and home (even if such notions are "boundlessly reconstituted" [Hall 2012: 24]). In other words, Bhabha's third space questions to a greater extent the primordiality—and possibility—of such concepts whether static or ever-changing.

As witnessed by Will, the way in which elements in the "serpentine flotation" (C: 475) are fused together in the trash island is reminiscent of both biological and industrial processes. Will envisions the island as an embryonic structure in the throes of giving birth at the same time as its movements are mechanized: "Rubbed, grated and clanked together" (C: 475). Once the island has settled into its new formation, it becomes an ecosystem that sustains its eclectic mishmash of plants both endemic and exotic to Australia: "Bobbing coconuts took root and grew into magnificent palm trees. Seedlings of mangrove, pandanus and coastal dune grasses came with the tides, other plants blew on board as seed, and none withered away" (C: 477). The temporal elasticity of Will's time on the island, where it is suggested he lived there for decades even though Hope (Will's wife) goes in search of him after being stranded by the cyclone for only forty days (Molloy 2012: 3), suggests a circularity inherent in Indigenous notions of life and land, in which nature becomes a connective tissue between past, present, and future. Yet the illusion of a new space of Indigenous sovereignty that remains untouched by colonial intervention cannot be sustained; Hope's determination to find Will and bring him back to what is left of Desperance effectively expels him from his self-made "paradise" (C: 477).

Bhabha's third space of enunciation departs from binarizing notions of culture, in which there is a clear delineation of authority between the colonizer and colonized. Instead, Bhabha emphasizes the emergence of hybrid knowledge and "a contingent, borderline experience [that] opens up *in-between* coloniser and colonised" (Bhabha [1994] 2004: 206; see also Dudgeon and Fielder 2006: 401). Hybridity is what constitutes the third space, where what emerges "at the intersection of different languages jousting for authority" (Bhabha 2009: x) is a translational site irreducible to binary logic and separation. The undecidability of cultural signs is perhaps best exemplified in Norm and Elias's discussions of constellations. Norm and Elias's fishing journeys show a site of negotiation involving resistance to and acceptance of knowledge from the other culture. On one of their fishing trips together, they describe the same phenomenon with two cosmologies that represent vastly different social and cultural values. For Norm, the morning star is known as "*yidimil*," a presentiment of misfortune for those who see her: "*She only comes for death*" (C: 91). However, for Elias, "She is Venus . . . who is also the beautiful Aphrodite from the sea" (C: 90). At first, these cosmologies appear totally irreconcilable; in Norm's Indigenous worldview, to gaze at *yidimil* is tantamount to one's demise, whereas for Elias, the morning star embodies the pleasure and beauty of the mythical goddess from ancient Rome and Greece. However, their conversation effects a new understanding of the constellation that operates across the divide between Western and Indigenous worldviews: The morning star is refigured as a seductress who not only pulls "heartbroken sailors and fishing men to her beauty" (*C*: 90) but also pulls them to their deaths.

Conclusion

In a 2004 interview that featured in the journal *Antipodes*, Jean-François Vernay asked Wright (2004: 122), "How do you perceive the reconciliation issue?" Wright's clipped answer "I don't perceive it!" tells us much about the author's judgment on white and Indigenous relations as she was composing *Carpentaria*. The novel takes inspiration from the contemporary struggle experienced by Aboriginal Australians to affirm their sovereignty over sacred land.[8] *Carpentaria* also shows the fractious relations between settler and Aboriginal communities through representing physical and symbolic violence committed by the former against the latter, including but not limited to dispossession, unlawful arrest, rape, and torture. Consequently, the novel puts little hope in the notion of reconciliation, instead appearing to celebrate the resilience of Aboriginal culture in spite of British colonization through the transmission of ancestral stories. Yet Wright's (2004) reply to Vernay also introduces a problem at the level of its composition and reception. Wright experienced a common dilemma for Aboriginal writers, which was how to utilize the language of the oppressors "without falling into the trap of 'thinking white,' or 'sounding white'" (Lowry 2008: para. 14). She overcame this problem through adopting a form that evokes the tradition of oral storytelling in Aboriginal culture. This strategy enabled her to write a novel that could escape "the colonising spider's trap door" (Wright 2007: 90) by communicating ancestral knowledge of the Dreaming "as though some old Aboriginal person was telling the story" (Wright 2007: 89). Yet it is precisely the orality of *Carpentaria* that leads some reviewers and publishers to criticize the novel as just a "rambling showing-off of [her] . . . literary skills" (Syson 2007: 85) or "too difficult stylistically" (Perlez 2007: para. 1) for the general reading public. However, as Ravenscroft (2010) has observed, Western readers grappling with Wright's unique style tend to domesticate its discomforting elements through reference

---

8. *Carpentaria* is dedicated to Murrandoo Yanner, an Indigenous activist who protested the development of the Century Zinc Mine in Queensland during the 1990s. The character of Will Phantom appears to be modeled on Yanner (Lowry 2008: para. 13), while the Gurfurritt Mine displays similarities to Century Zinc.

to magic realism and canonical figures from Australian literature, principally Xavier Herbert. In this article, I have argued that *Carpentaria* sits uneasily in a canon of Great Australian Novels despite repeated attempts by scholars and reviewers to justify their inclusion of it on the grounds of formal innovation, genealogical resemblance, and narrative maximality. The reason for my argument against such inclusion is that for Buell (2008), GANs begin with "the postulate of each nation speaking in its own voice within and against which its writers must thereafter contend" (133). It is my contention that Wright's vision of the Australian nation in its current form is divided, rather than unified, in its voice and politics. I have therefore argued in this article that *Carpentaria* imagines the future of Indigenous sovereignty as being neither totally separate from nor harmonized with the surrounding white settler culture of Australia. *Carpentaria* shows the resilience of Indigenous knowledge even as it is subject to transformation upon contact with other ideological and epistemological frameworks. Bhabha's third space is instrumental to understanding Wright's literary project, which is to show how negotiation between Aboriginal and settler cultures produces a radical and hybrid site that simultaneously invites antagonism as well as shared understanding between the two.

Liz Shek-Noble, PhD, is a project assistant professor in the Center for Global Communication Strategies at the University of Tokyo. Her research areas include literary and media disability studies, contemporary Australian literature, and literary bioethics. Her work has appeared in publications including the *Journal of the Association for the Study of Australian Literature, Disability and Society*, and the *Journal of Literary and Cultural Disability Studies*. She is currently working on a multiyear project about cultural representations of disability in contemporary Australia and is coediting a special issue of the *Journal of Literary and Cultural Disability Studies* on intersections between disability studies and critical animal studies.

Works Cited

Ashcroft, Bill. 2009. "Caliban's Voice: Writing in the Third Space." In Ikas and Wagner 2009a: 107–22.
Ashcroft, Bill, Gareth Griffiths, and Helen Tiffin. (1989) 2002. *The Empire Writes Back: Theory and Practice in Post-colonial Literatures*. London: Routledge.

Atkinson, Meera. 2013. *"Carpentaria." Reading Australia.* readingaustralia.com.au /essays/carpentaria/.

Bhabha, Homi. (1994) 2004. *The Location of Culture.* London: Routledge.

Bhabha, Homi. 2009. "In the Cave of Making: Thoughts on Third Space." In Ikas and Wagner 2009a: ix–xiv.

Brewster, Anne. 2010. "Indigenous Sovereignty and the Crisis of Whiteness in Alexis Wright's *Carpentaria." Australian Literary Studies* 25, no. 4: 85–100.

Buell, Lawrence. 2008. "The Unkillable Dream of the Great American Novel: Moby-Dick as Test Case." *American Literary History* 20, nos. 1–2: 132–55. doi .org/10.1093/alh/ajn005.

Buell, Lawrence. 2014. *The Dream of the Great American Novel.* Cambridge, MA: Belknap Press of Harvard University Press.

Conor, Liz, and Ann McGrath. 2017. "Xavier Herbert: Forgotten or Repressed?" *Cultural Studies Review* 23, no. 2: 62–69. doi.org/10.5130/csr.v23i2.5818.

Devlin-Glass, Frances. 2008. "A Politics of the Dreamtime: Destructive and Regenerative Rainbows in Alexis Wright's *Carpentaria." Australian Literary Studies* 23, no. 4: 392–407. doi.org/10.20314/als.db10692a2e.

Dixon, Robert. 2005. "Tim Winton, *Cloudstreet*, and the Field of Australian Literature." *Westerly* 50: 245–60.

Dudgeon, Pat, and John Fielder. 2006. "Third Spaces within Tertiary Places: Indigenous Australian Studies." *Journal of Community and Applied Social Psychology* 16, no. 5: 396–409. doi.org/10.1002/casp.883.

Elder, Catriona. (2007) 2020. *Being Australian: Narratives of National Identity.* London: Routledge.

Ferrier, Carole. 2006. "The Best Australian Novel for Years . . ." *Hecate's Australian Women's Book Review* 18, no. 2: 20–21.

Foucault, Michel. 1986. "Of Other Spaces." *Diacritics* 16, no. 1: 22–27. doi.org/10.2307 /464648.

Gibson, Chris, Susan Luckman, and Julie Willoughby-Smith. 2010. "Creativity without Borders? Rethinking Remoteness and Proximity." *Australian Geographer* 41, no. 1: 25–38. doi.org/10.1080/00049180903535543.

Gleeson-White, Jane. 2013. "Capitalism versus the Agency of Place: An Ecocritical Reading of *That Deadman Dance* and *Carpentaria." Journal of the Association for the Study of Australian Literature* 13, no. 2. openjournals.library.sydney.edu .au/index.php/JASAL/article/view/9867/9756.

Hall, Demelza. 2012. "The Isle of Refuse in Alexis Wright's *Carpentaria*: Reconstituting Heterotopic Space." *Southerly* 72, no. 3: 12–26.

Heiss, Anita M. 2003. *Dhuuluu-Yala: To Talk Straight.* Canberra: Aboriginal Studies Press.

Heiss, Anita, and Peter Minter, eds. 2008. *Macquarie PEN Anthology of Aboriginal Literature.* Crows Nest, NSW: Allen and Unwin.

Herbert, Xavier. (1939) 2008. *Capricornia*. London: HarperCollins.

Holgate, Ben. 2015. "Unsettling Narratives: Re-evaluating Magical Realism as Post-colonial Discourse through Alexis Wright's *Carpentaria* and *The Swan Book*." *Journal of Postcolonial Writing* 51, no. 6: 634–47. doi.org/10.1080/17449855.2015.1105856.

Ikas, Karin, and Gerhard Wagner, eds. 2009a. *Communicating in the Third Space*. London: Routledge.

Ikas, Karin, and Gerhard Wagner. 2009b. Introduction to Ikas and Wagner 2009a: 1–7.

Jose, Nicholas, ed. 2009. *The Literature of Australia: An Anthology*. New York: W. W. Norton.

Joseph, Laura. 2009. "Dreaming Phantoms and Golems: Elements of the Place Beyond Nation in *Carpentaria* and *Dreamhunter*." In "Australian Literature in the Global World," edited by Wenche Ommundsen and Tony Simoes da Silva. Special issue, *Journal of the Association for the Study of Australian Literature*: 1–10.

Lowry, Elizabeth. 2008. "The Fishman Lives the Lore." *London Review of Books* 30, no. 8. www.lrb.co.uk/v30/n08/lowr01.html.

Meyer, Angela. 2009. "Meeting Alex Miller, Part Three: On Cross-Eyed Novels, the Time We Have, and Liberties of Language." *Crikey*, December 15. blogs.crikey.com.au/literaryminded/2009/12/15/meeting-alex-miller-part-three-on-cross-eyed-novels-the-time-we-have-and-liberties-of-language/.

Molloy, Diane. 2012. "Finding Hope in the Stories: Alexis Wright's *Carpentaria* and the Carnivalesque Search for a New Order." *Journal of the Association for the Study of Australian Literature* 12, no. 3: 1–8.

Perche, Diana. 2017. "Ten Years On, It's Time We Learned the Lessons from the Failed Northern Territory Intervention." *Conversation*, June 26. theconversation.com/ten-years-on-its-time-we-learned-the-lessons-from-the-failed-northern-territory-intervention-79198.

Perlez, Jane. 2007. "Essay: Aboriginal Lit." *New York Times*, November 18. www.nytimes.com/2007/11/18/books/review/Perlez-t.html.

Polak, Iva. 2017. *Futuristic Worlds in Australian Aboriginal Fiction*. Oxford: Peter Lang.

Ravenscroft, Alison. 2010. "Dreaming of Others: *Carpentaria* and Its Critics." *Cultural Studies Review* 16, no. 2: 194–224. doi.org/10.5130/csr.v16i2.1700.

Renes, Cornelis Martin. 2019. "Sung by an Indigenous Siren: Epic and Epistemology in Alexis Wright's *Carpentaria*." *Coolabah*, no. 27: 52–71. doi.org/10.1344/co20192752-71.

Rodoreda, Geoff. 2017. "Orality and Narrative Structure in Alexis Wright's *Carpentaria*." *Journal of the Association for the Study of Australian Literature* 16, no. 2: 1–14.

Rutherford, Jonathan. 1990. "The Third Space: Interview with Homi Bhabha." In *Identity, Community, Culture, Difference*, edited by Jonathan Rutherford, 207–21. London: Lawrence and Wishart.

Seran, Justine. 2013. "Fortunes and Fringe-Dwellers in Australian Aboriginal Literature: Alexis Wright's *Carpentaria*." *Australian Studies*, no. 5: 1–15.

Sharp, Nonie. 2007. Review of *Carpentaria*, by Alexis Wright. *Island*, no. 111: 61–67.

Sharrad, Paul. 2009. "Beyond Capricornia: Ambiguous Promise in Alexis Wright." *Australian Literary Studies* 24, no. 1: 52–65. doi.org/10.20314/als.299450cf39.

Shoemaker, Adam. 2008. "Hard Dreams and Indigenous Worlds in Australia's North." *Hecate* 34, no. 1: 55–61.

Stewart, Ken. 1983. "Life and Death of the Bunyip: History and the 'Great Australian Novel.'" *Westerly* 28, no. 2: 39–44.

Syson, Ian. 2007. "Uncertain Magic." *Overland*, no. 187: 85–86.

Wheeler, Belinda. 2013. "Introduction—the Emerging Canon." In *A Companion to Australian Aboriginal Literature*, edited by Belinda Wheeler, 1–13. Rochester, NY: Camden House.

Winch, Tara June. 2020. "The Australian Book You've Finally Got Time For: *Carpentaria* by Alexis Wright." *Guardian*, June 3. www.theguardian.com/books/2020/jun/04/the-australian-book-youve-finally-got-time-for-carpentaria-by-alexis-wright.

Wright, Alexis. 1997. *Plains of Promise*. Brisbane: University of Queensland Press.

Wright, Alexis. 1998. "Breaking Taboos." *Australian Humanities Review*, no. 11. australianhumanitiesreview.org/1998/09/01/breaking-taboos/.

Wright, Alexis. 2002. "Politics of Writing." *Southerly* 62, no. 2: 10–20.

Wright, Alexis. 2004. Interview by Jean-François Vernay. *Antipodes* 18, no. 2: 119–22.

Wright, Alexis. (2006) 2009. *Carpentaria*. London: Constable.

Wright, Alexis. 2007. "On Writing *Carpentaria*." In "Harper's Gold," edited by Ivor Indyk. Special issue, *Heat*, no. 13: 79–95.

Wright, Alexis. 2013. *The Swan Book*. Sydney: Giramondo.

Wright, Alexis. 2017. "The Big Book about Small Town Australia That Travelled the World." *Guardian*, September 7. www.theguardian.com/culture/2017/sep/08/the-big-book-about-small-town-australia-that-travelled-the-world.

Young, Robert J. C. 2009. "The Void of Misgiving." In Ikas and Wagner 2009a: 81–95.

Madeleine Thien's Chinese Encyclopedia: Facts, Musics, Sympathies

IVAN DELAZARI

"Novels are long," Franco Moretti (2013: 165) reminds us, because they comprise series of adventures. Not all novels are "big" and "ambitious," though. James Wood's (2000) review of Zadie Smith's *White Teeth* assigns the two adjectives and the label *hysterical realism* to only a number of contemporary fictions, which literature scholars would qualify as "encyclopedic" (Kyllönen 2018), "maximalist" (Ercolino 2012), "systems" (LeClair 1987), and "Mega-Novels" (Karl 1985; Letzler 2017). In that genre constellation, chains of adventures begin to read as somewhat dysfunctional either because they grow overabundant or due to deliberate insertion of superfluous information that retards narrative pace and reduces plausibility. Despite certain efforts to admit or reinstate women's novels as tokens of such fiction,[1] maximalist writing remains predominantly male (Letzler 2017: 26) and restrictive in its adoption of generic features.

In many ways, the inertia dates back to Edward Mendelson's (1976) normative definition of *encyclopedic narrative*, which tries to limit the entire selection to one champion work per nation. The point of my article, however, is not to prove that Madeleine Thien's *Do Not Say We Have Nothing* (2016) is or is not encyclopedic or maximalist. Instead, looking at this impressive prose work by an Asian Canadian author set in the People's Republic of China, I hope to high-

This research was supported by the Basic Research Program at the National Research University Higher School of Economics in 2020. I am grateful to Dr. Jason S. Polley for referring me to Madeleine Thien's novel and inviting me to teach it at Hong Kong Baptist University in the spring of 2018. I dedicate this article to my students.

1. See Kasia Boddy's (2019) discussion of recent female writers' contributions to the related genre set of "Great American Novels."

Genre, Vol. 54, No. 2   July 2021
DOI 10.1215/00166928-9263078   © 2021 by University of Oklahoma

light a property that is at least partly responsible for the readerly illusion of a comprehensive data coverage at the core of the *fiction as encyclopedia* metaphor. When, for instance, the nineteenth-century Russian critic Vissarion Belinsky (1974: 181) dubs Alexander Pushkin's novel in verse *Eugene Onegin* (*Evgenii Onegin*, 1833) "an encyclopedia of Russian life," he is delighted by both how *much*, quantitatively, Pushkin "managed to express and imply" about "the world of Russian nature, the world of Russian society" and how crucially Pushkin's masterwork affected its contemporaries. No matter how laconic Pushkin's poetic diction may be, the reader perceives the text-world as fundamentally complete. In Marie-Laure Ryan's (2019: 75) storyworld theory, this default setting of literary mimetism rests on readerly immersion: "While we don't know how many children Lady Macbeth had, and we will never know, we still regard her as somebody who had a determinate number of children. It's just that the text does not specify this number. We consequently treat it as missing information, rather than as ontological gap." Feeling that a narrative is "encyclopedic"—that is, comprehensively detailed—may depend on the evocativeness of metonymic implication: those elements of the storyworld that are explicitly signified suggest others that surround them so convincingly that the absent facts appear to be covered, as if in another "entry" of the text.

Both Belinsky's 1845 and Mendelson's 1976 notions of a literary encyclopedia are strictly national. Mendelson (1976: 1267–68) surveys Western literatures to find a single encyclopedic author in each, one that would "occupy a special historical position" in his or her respective culture and expose "the whole social and linguistic range of his [sic] nation." The exception Mendelson makes for America by adding Thomas Pynchon on top of Herman Melville reflects his intuition that literary monocultures are at the threshold of globalist dissolution, with a new world literature being born. However, his coronation of Pynchon as "the encyclopedist of that newly-forming international culture" (1271) insistently retains the article *the* instead of *an*. On Mendelson's essentialist terms, Thien's case would be highly suspicious, since *she* stands so articulately not *within* a national language and literature but on the border *in-between*. She is a Canadian (Western) author of Malay-Chinese (Eastern) ethnic background writing a transpacific novel in English, with multiple use of Chinese characters (in both senses of the word), about the century-long traumatic turmoil of revolutionary China narrated as a family saga. "Pynchon's new internationalism" (Mendelson 1976:

1272) is an elegant formulation, but Thien's 2016 title appears to announce a more aptly internationalist case than the one Mendelson envisions and celebrates in Pynchon's *Gravity's Rainbow* (1973). "Do not say we have nothing" is a back translation of a line from the Chinese translation of a Russian translation of the French original of the communist anthem *Internationale* (see Thien 2016: 438), so the title is resonant not only with the twenty-first-century state of global affairs but also with transcultural claims of encyclopedism. In their wish to account for everything, encyclopedias aspire to trespass beyond national(ist) realms, even though they indeed "render the full range of knowledge and beliefs of a national culture, while identifying the ideological perspectives from which that culture shapes and interprets its knowledge" (Mendelson 1976: 1269). With Thien, it is just no longer obvious *which*, or *whose*, culture is at stake as the reference point: is hers a Chinese encyclopedia or a Canadian encyclopedia of China?

The diverse range of facts and attitudes that Thien's novel embraces lets it stand on both shores as a text that is *inherently comparative*. Due to its structure of plot and values, the book may supply a comparative literature scholar with a sufficient range of issues across national, medial, epistemological, and affective borders to seek no second counterpart for comparative analysis: instead of reading a Canadian *and* a Chinese novel, we may just read Thien. This is not to say that *Do Not Say We Have Nothing* itself draws analytic comparisons between or builds up a scientific typology of the recent phenomena in the East-West cultural histories. Yet the novel is inherently comparative in the kind of metaphorical terms we may recognize as informationally and emotionally comprehensive— the goal of comparative literature that Edward Said ([1993] 1994: 32) celebrates in *Culture and Imperialism*:

> A comparative or, better, a contrapuntal perspective is required in order to see a connection between coronation rituals in England and the Indian durbars of the late nineteenth century. That is, we must be able to think through and interpret together experiences that are discrepant, each with its particular agenda and pace of development, its own internal formations, its internal coherence and system of external relationships, all of them coexisting and interacting with others.

To a similar end, Thien's "encyclopedia" employs music metonymically—as a subject matter in her storyworld—and metaphorically—as a model of narrative presentation associated with contrapuntal polyphony. Several melodic streams of equal importance scored in a piece by Johann Sebastian Bach—"Bā Hè" in Chinese (Thien 2016: 314)—are presented simultaneously, teaching the listener to segregate them gradually by parsing them into consequent little fragments and switching attention between those to end up integrating a mental polyphonic whole (see Delazari 2019).

Bits of contrapuntal streams may not be as logically consistent, explicitly referred to, and complete as entries in a perfect reference book about China, but Thien's narrative encyclopedism is different from the Belinsky/Mendelson national, closed-system type. Multiple intermingling characters and subplots, some of them dissonant, aborted, or redundant from Wood's (2000) aesthetic perspective,[2] enable us to experience the *worldlikeness*[3] of the novel in comparative and/as contrapuntal terms, with "discrepant," incompatible, and diverse agendas meeting in the reader's affective engagement with Thien's patchwork storyworld.

Do Not Say We Have Nothing opens with two Chinese ideograms translated as "family, household" and "record, register, music score," followed by two family trees listing the novel's characters (Thien 2016: iv). Thien's paratexts also include four epigraphs, two documentary photographic images, and fifty endnotes acknowledging her cited material. There are samples of Western (14) and Chinese "jianpu" (33) musical notation in chapter 1, as well as many Chinese words, in traditional or simplified characters and pinyin, throughout the book. The primary narrator, Marie, alias Jiang Li-Ling, starts by sharing her early memories of her late father, Jiang Kai, a mainland Chinese ex-concert pianist who in 1978 defects to Canada, where Marie is born in 1979. Kai commits suicide in Hong Kong during the 1989 Tiananmen Square protests in Beijing, where his beloved friend and music mentor Sparrow is gunned down in the streets by the People's Liberation Army. Sparrow's eighteen-year-old daughter Ai-Ming, who joins the students in the Square, flees the PRC in 1990 and stays temporarily in Vancouver with Marie and Ma (Marie's mother). Ai-Ming moves on to seek refuge in the United States but interrupts her stay just before her legalization is due and flies back to China for her mother's funeral in 1996. Ai-Ming's trace is lost in 1998. In 2016, Marie—now a thirty-seven-year-old college mathematician—compiles a broad and nuanced narrative of three generations of Ai-Ming's family from Ai-Ming's

---

2. The abundance of superfluous storylines is one of the principal symptoms of "hysterical realism" in the critical diagnoses Wood (2000) gives to such novelists as Zadie Smith, Salman Rushdie, and Don DeLillo.

3. Unlike the logical foundations of modern Western encyclopedias, "the worldlikeness of narrative arises from its capacity to evoke the patterns of interaction that accompany our engagement with a world that . . . first emerges in a process of embodied exploration (and only later on may be conceptualized as an autonomous domain preexisting the subject)" (Caracciolo 2019: 116).

and Ma's fragmented stories and from her own later conversations with several people during her trip to Shanghai and Hong Kong. Via Kai and Ai-Ming, that family narrative intertwines with her own. Thien's resulting "repository of unofficial history" (Patterson, Polley, and Thien 2017) covers the Chinese Civil War (1946–1949) and establishment of communist China, the Land Reform and famine of the early 1950s, the Hundred Flowers Campaign (1956) and the Great Leap Forward (1958–1962), the Cultural Revolution (1966–1976), and the Tiananmen Square movement (1989). The life of Sparrow, who was born in 1940 and killed in 1989, boomerangs between the first and the last chapters, alongside the lives of his Communist Party musician father Ba Lute and his wise Big Mother Knife, his politically prosecuted aunt Swirl and her resistant prison escapee husband Wen the Dreamer, their exceptionally talented violinist daughter—Sparrow's niece Zhuli, who hangs herself in the face of Red Guards' violence—and so many more. Sparrow is a composer and professor at the Shanghai Conservatory of Music, where Zhuli and Kai study during its 1966 vandalistic closedown for the Cultural Revolution. Images of Western symphony and chamber music provide the events with a permanent counterpoint of sounds and silences, well after Zhuli is dead and Sparrow is forced to abandon music for factory assemblage of wooden crates, electric bulbs, and small radios—first in Guangxi Province, then in Beijing.

Thien pours showers of information on her reader, which is especially challenging for those who know little about the historical contexts accommodating her characters' lives. To others, certain problems arise with relating the information in the novel to the China they know from elsewhere. The central argument in what follows is that Thien's novel is *not* a conventional encyclopedia used as a reference source of organized factual knowledge about the world, but it does teach us to maintain Said's comparative, i.e., contrapuntal, perspective on facts, which might be wiser and wider than the Western rationalist stance, and engage with them sympathetically, for which music is an excellent model.

Facts

Expanding Mendelson's notion of encyclopedic narrative to comprise more texts than just one or two per nation, Frederick R. Karl (1985: 250) points out an entire "elitist" class of post–Second World War American "Mega-Novels." Stefano Ercolino's (2012) later modification of roughly the same genre combines recognition of postwar US origins of the *maximalist novel* with a discovery of its samples in contemporary Europe. Typical of postmodern taxonomies, his listing of its features—"length, encyclopedic mode, dissonant chorality, diegetic exuberance, completeness, narratorial omniscience, paranoid imagination, inter-semiocity, ethical commitment, and hybrid realism" (242)—sounds slightly Borgesian, as some categories overlap and even include one another. Decades earlier, Jorge Luis Borges ([1964] 1975: 103) famously ascribes this kind of thinking to an apocryphal "Chinese encyclopedia" that subdivides animals "into (a) those that belong to the Emperor, (b) embalmed ones, (c) those that are trained, (d) suckling pigs, (e) mermaids, (f) fabulous ones, (g) stray dogs, (h) those that are included in this classification, (i) those that tremble as if they were mad," and so forth. Defining encyclopedic novels in what may be read as an encyclopedia entry on such novels in the volume on *Reading Today*, Vesa Kyllönen (2018) titles his essay "Information and the Illusion of Totality," as though alerted by Borges's same novella. To excuse the logical flaws of the "Chinese encyclopedia," Borges ([1964] 1975: 104) remarks: "There is no classification of the universe that is not arbitrary and conjectural. The reason is very simple: we do not know what the universe is." Thien's *Do Not Say We Have Nothing* endorses this epistemological insight in that its cross-referential "entries" on life in China from the mid-twentieth to early twenty-first century do not exclude overlaps, repetitions, silences, circularities, and errors à la Borges. It is worth recalling, though, that uncontroversial, positivist descriptions of the world result from reductive silencing of phenomena that do not fit into a classificatory grid. The West's ignorance about and Orientalist appropriation of the East exemplify this unifying, homophonic ordering.

The idea that the world is incomplete and that literature is not *world* literature until the Orient is taken into account is characteristic of the Eurocentric vision still manifest in Johann Wolfgang von Goethe's celebrated announcement of *Weltliteratur* on January 31, 1827. Enthusiastically reading "a Chinese novel," Goethe ([1906] 1984: 132–33) informs Johann Peter Eckermann that "the Chinamen think, act, and feel almost exactly like us" and articulates several insightful observations about classical Chinese fiction. Even though Goethe is slightly amazed with "an infinite number of legends which are constantly introduced into the narrative" in the book he is reading, it does not strike him as much as Borges's "Chinese encyclopedia" strikes Michel Foucault at the opening of *The Order of Things*. The "exotic charm of another system of thought" (Foucault [1966] 1994: iv), which Goethe expects but is reassured *not* to find in the German translation of the Chinese novel, is laid bare in Borges's notorious taxonomy. At the same time, China, "whose name alone constitutes for the West a vast reservoir of Utopias" (Foucault [1966] 1994: viii), is in Borges's as well as Goethe's presentation strangely akin to some past aspects of European experience. In his "archaeology," Foucault uncovers the premodern—preclassical, in Foucault's terminology—episteme and comments on how pre-Enlightenment encyclopedias would not resort to alphabetical ordering of entries (which would be arbitrary but consistent from a modern perspective). Instead, their manner of presenting items in what may seem quite a Borgesian succession rests on the idea of fundamental similitude, even equivalence, between reality and language. Foucault ([1966] 1994: 37) points out the tendency of late sixteenth- to early seventeenth-century encyclopedias "not to reflect what one knows in the neutral element of language . . . but to reconstitute the very order of the universe by the way in which words are linked together and arranged in space." The resulting compendium certainly looks chaotic from our standard view on encyclopedism. Arranged by analogy to circles and trees, facts are organized into "a space that would be at once an Encyclopaedia and a Library"—both the content and the container, with words distributed "according to the forms of adjacency, kinship, analogy, and subordination prescribed by the world itself" (36–37). After this perfect isomorphism of linguistic signs and real objects disintegrates in the classical period of the seventeenth and eighteenth centuries, only poetic diction—the "art of language"—sustains it in its "counter-discourse" displaced from the system of rational thought (42–43).

Literature is therefore a perfect meeting point of the old and the new, of East and West as asynchronous civilizations coexisting in contrapuntal simultaneity: in the nineteenth and twentieth centuries, discursive "Chineseness" of a Borgesian type—one that piles unnecessary details with no apparent motivation—is comprehensible to Goethe and Foucault because, through comparison, they recognize it as, or retranslate it into, some archaic mode of Europeanness. The divorce of life from language results in a "Library of the Universe"—an identical twin to Borges's "Library of Babel," although Foucault ([1966] 1994: 84) cites Charles Bonnet this time, not Borges. In that "Library," the entire world is encased in a superbook—the encyclopedia, in which everything is described. It is no surprise that in another Borges story this all-inclusive superbook acquires the form of a *Chinese* novel—a narrative maze whose "forking paths" of alternative possibilities, which the course of events (Moretti's *adventures*) may potentially take from any point in time, are presented in single file. This plot appears so "cha-otic" (Borges [1944] 1993: 75) that even the novelist's descendants fail to grasp its construction principle. Ts'ui Pên's narrative is mistaken for "a shapeless mass of contradictory rough drafts" with the hero dying "in the third chapter, while in the fourth he is alive" (74). Characteristically, it takes a British Orientalist to solve the charade: the novel aspires to absorb and work through *all* alternative scenarios, which multiply at each juncture. Hence its analogy to a "Platonic hereditary work, passed on from father to son, to which each individual would add a new chapter or correct, with pious care, the work of his elders" (74). This infinite poly-plot narrative is yet another "Chinese encyclopedia," with neither beginning nor end, whose readable bits and pieces suffice to denote its forever-deferred whole.

In a sense, Ts'ui Pên's novel is a radical amplification of some features of Chinese writing that Goethe notices. When Moretti (2013: 230–40) subjects Chi-nese novels to digitalized distant reading, his findings reveal much less similar-ity between Eastern and Western narrative manners than Goethe's nineteenth-century observations did.

Drawing an important etymological distinction between verse and prose, Moretti reminds us that the latter "is not symmetrical, and this immediately cre-ates a sense of impermanence and irreversibility: prose, *provorsa*: forward-look-ing" suggests that "the text has an orientation, it leans forwards" (162). Unlike verse, where each line "can to a certain extent stand alone," "prose is continuous" (163). Its forward-leaning narrativity determines the course of the Western novel. But since "east Asian and west European novels developed independently of each other" as though in two isolated and distant natural "laboratories" (168), Chinese novels, with their massive character systems and plot variability, afford "all sorts of sequels" (169) to each single event, which makes them genuinely different from their literary counterparts in England and France. Instead of unfolding adventure sequences, Chinese novels are busy "*preventing* developments" and "minimiz-ing narrativity" across thousands of pages. Cao Xueqin's *The Story of the Stone*, a.k.a. *Dream of the Red Chamber*, in Moretti's (2013: 169–70) report, "realizes a 'horizontal' dominant, where what really matters is not what lies 'ahead' of a given event . . . but what lies 'to the side' of it." That is, "in every chapter of the novel its huge pack of characters is re-shuffled, the new 'hand' forms new character-clusters, which generate new features in the figures we already knew" (239). The nonlinear "architecture" of Chinese novels, which is captured in Borges's perplexing novel-labyrinth, makes them "really an alternative" but "*comparable*" tradition in relation to Western writing (170).

Thien's *Do Not Say We Have Nothing* refers explicitly to neither classical Chinese novels nor Borges's fictional encyclopedias and forking narratives. However, its character range is extensive while its chronologies are mixed, life stories unfinished, and historical facts presented in patchwork portions. Marie does impose order on the narratives she recycles, but she does not untwine them to single out the uniform storyline or delete unimportant themes and characters. Instead, she keeps them in contrapuntal, ongoing motion, building connective networks among them. In Marie and Ai-Ming's family trees drawn at the beginning of the novel, none of the characters who die in the course of the narrated events has a second date next to their names: Zhuli, Sparrow, and Kai are all born only, as if the facts of their deaths are not fully established. The option of reading only some uncollected parts of *Do Not Say We Have Nothing*, in a random order, appeals to the author: "I would love to see the novel published much like the Book of Records, in its different chapters. This is how history comes to us, in bits and pieces out of order" (Lee 2019: 27).

In Thien, "the Book of Records" is a handwritten novel, whose few opening sections Wen the Dreamer locates in a book shop shortly before he marries Swirl. Wen begins collecting and copying chapters of the book, but soon he is unable to find any beyond chapter 31, so he begins composing himself. The Book of Records haunts Thien's novel, coming up on numerous occasions to supplement its many narrative progressions with an extra bunch of characters and events told and retold variedly to interrupt Marie's weaving of her accumulated subplots, whenever she or one of her characters happens to get hold of yet another chapter of the Book of Records.

Marie's secondhand stories are explicitly meant to become part of a larger Book of Records, which is compiled into an indefinite number of copies by a collective, anonymous body of scribes, an unauthored and unpublished volume reporting facts beyond the reach of officially documented history. However, Marie thinks about this larger book as just the same Book of Records whose chapter 17 she possesses—the one in Sparrow's neat calligraphic handwriting, which she inherited from Kai. "It is a simple thing to write a book," Marie tells us toward the end of the novel. "Simpler, too, when the book already exists, and has been passed from person to person, in different versions, permutations and variations" (Thien 2016: 462): the Book of Records paradoxically encapsulates the very narrative that it is part of, because there is no reason why Marie, or anyone else, should not supplement it with the very story we are reading. The Book of Records thus has neither a master copy nor even one single (national) language: Marie knows too little Chinese, so she tells her story in English. The potentially endless Chinese encyclopedia-novel of Borges and the Library of the Universe of Bonnet/Foucault as well as the international and multilingual comparative synchronization of Said's counterpoint of cultures are fulfilled in *Do Not Say We Have Nothing.*

The "initial" chapters of the Book of Records, which its Chinese copyists such as Wen the Dreamer and then Swirl and Big Mother Knife slightly modify in order to pass secret messages between each other—for example, encrypting the date and place of Swirl's post–labor camp reunion with Wen (308)—acquire alternative, forking plots. The Book of Records can contain an infinite number of versions of what happens to its protagonists Da-Wei and May Fourth from chapter 31 onward: while Wen writes his own experiences into Da-Wei's and May's, other readers and copyists are free to act accordingly. There can be two chapters 32, two chapters 33, and so forth—potentially, any number of each.

With Marie's story about Ai-Ming in British Columbia and Sparrow, Zhuli, Kai, and all others in Shanghai, what we read in Thien is a transpacific Book of Records, a narrative Wikipedia open to editing, and a bicultural catalogue of the Library of Babel. The project of adding records is personal for each contributor but totally devoid of individualist ambition, as each name and experience is fictionalized with no claims for the national encyclopedic narrative. Wen the Dreamer, Sparrow, and Marie are not Pushkin, Melville, and Pynchon; nor is the author, Madeleine Thien. They are all more like Ishmael sharing his knowledge of whales—factual, historical, scientific, and fictional—for the reader to handle comparatively. Rescuing the Thien characters from the oblivious nothingness that official history secures them is not only the narrator's job but the reader's as well. Jiang Kai, for instance, as early as in the opening chapter, is a pile of scores and diaries (Thien 2016: 5–6), a textual entity. Marie is even unable to locate his grave in Hong Kong, just as Ling (Sparrow's wife) and her daughter Ai-Ming cannot be sure that they have reclaimed Sparrow's, not someone or something else's, ashes from the Beijing authorities. After Marie lets her late father into her story, Kai lives on as a record.

Marie gets to know the Book of Records starting from its chapter 17. A book of this kind can be read from any page in the middle: after all, who reads encyclopedias from cover to cover? Alphabetic or chronological, narrative or descriptive, factual or fictional, the Book of Records is beginningless and endless. Records are just kept, passing through copyists, compilers, and crafters of various sequels. The parts we get to learn from the "original" Book of Records in the Thien storyworld are always copies of copies: there is a detailed rendition of chapter 42 (334–36), for instance—in Marie's English approximation of Wen the Dreamer's version of a May Fourth and Da-Wei adventure, which is based on some untraceable personal experience of Wen's. Like Wen the Dreamer's, Marie's transformation from recipient to producer of records is natural: "In my dreams, the Book of Records continued" (88). It is not *I continued the Book of Records*, though: the Book is "ever-expanding" (199), self-propelled.

In quantificational diagrams of novelistic plots, Moretti (2013: 230–40) shows how, on a chapter-size scale visualization, a Charles Dickens narrative looks perfectly symmetrical, whereas a Chinese novel does not—due to the bigger number of interconnected characters and delayed narrative unfoldment. Symmetry is achieved on a much larger scale, when one registers the recurrent episodic patterns of poetic—rhymelike—similitudes in Chinese novels at hundreds of pages' distance from one another. Some asymmetries of the Thien novel result from the fact that *Do Not Say We Have Nothing*, despite its considerable length and scope, is itself a fragment to be continued: "In my mind, Ai-Ming's story has a hundred possible endings" (Thien 2016: 453). Analogies, similitudes, polysemies, symbolic correspondences, and translational equivalences that tie the novel together are neither Western rationalist nor classical Chinese. It is by the chance to compare the two alternating cultural stances and narrative traditions that the book mobilizes its reader's mind and feelings.

Musics

Numerous references to music—mostly Western art music, but also several Chinese tunes—are not an arrogant demonstration of the author's encyclopedic erudition. Turning *Do Not Say We Have Nothing*—the title that itself alludes to an internationally known song—into a book of *music* records, they encourage those of us who are familiar with the way they sound to immerse ourselves in Thien's storyworld more intensively, while everyone else should develop an "urge to listen" to the novel's virtual soundtrack (see Delazari 2021).

Among Ercolino's (2012: 242–43) genre indicators of the maximalist novel, there are "inter-semiocity"—the tendency to employ other sign systems, such as painting or cinema—and "dissonant chorality" defined as "a peculiar interweaving of chorality and polyphony" (246), whereupon none of the multiple narrative voices and/or characters dominates the plot. Emily Petermann (2014), in her study *The Musical Novel*, uses the more conventional term *intermediality* for inter-semiocity and illustrates the phenomenon with a whole series of contemporary novels centered on J. S. Bach's *Goldberg Variations* (*Goldberg-Variationen*, 1741). Bach's composition, written for the harpsichord in theme-and-variations form and made extremely popular for the late twentieth century by the Canadian star pianist Glenn Gould, is, like many other Bach classics, a signature masterpiece of Western polyphony. *Do Not Say We Have Nothing* could provide yet another *Goldberg* case for Petermann: according to Thien, "It's not an understatement to say that *Goldberg Variations* created this book" (Lee 2019: 19).

Not only do Thien's characters listen to Bach's music recurrently, but also the narrative layout of *Do Not Say We Have Nothing* speaks directly to the *Goldbergs*. As Thien explains,

> It starts with a simple story—Ai-Ming arrives and begins to tell this story to Marie, but it begins in a simple way because Marie is still a child. The listener, at first, is a child. So it starts like the *Goldberg Variations*, a simple melody, a simple theme, and like the *Goldberg Variations*, that simple theme is reworked into increasingly complex variations and canons until we return back to the ending which is the beginning, the very same aria as at the beginning. But by the time we get back to the aria, that theme has been opened up into such a spectrum of human emotions and human experience, from playfulness to joy to giddiness, an almost dance-like quality, all the way to profound grief and sorrow. (Patterson, Polley, and Thien 2017)

The novel's trajectory from the narrator's autobiographical theme in part 1, chapter 1, and back to it in the "Coda," imitates Bach's cyclic pattern of aria—thirty variations—aria again. Among what we might call Bach's musical "encyclopedias"—big, ambitious keyboard cycles that explore the possibilities of contrapuntal polyphony and aspire to exhaustively take all the tonal directions the Western chromatic scale offers in the tonal idiom, such as *The Well-Tempered Clavier* (*Das wohltemperierte Klavier*, 1722) and *The Art of Fugue* (*Die Kunst der Fuge*, 1751)—the *Goldberg Variations* is the briefest and clearest.

As Petermann reminds us, the "theme" to be varied in Bach is in fact *not* the simple melody played in the aria's right-hand part but the bass line in the left hand, which establishes the harmonic progression. The theme itself, therefore, "is actually never stated in isolation," while the aria is already "its first variation" (Petermann 2014: 150). By way of analogy, Marie's story opening *Do Not Say We Have Nothing* is the first variation of the theme underlying stories told further in the book as their common denominator.

Bach's theme in the bass is the formal foundation that a nonexpert listener learns gradually to hear in all variations, after many listenings and without even being aware of it because it is so basic that we may not recognize it as a self-contained melody: it appears to serve as just the accompaniment, the continuo whose role is shadowed by the more interesting melody in the higher register. This underestimation of the bass line is typical of Western audiences starting from the classical period, when Baroque contrapuntal polyphony stating the equal "rights" of its simultaneously played parts was replaced with the homophonic principle of harmony in the accompaniment plus the main melody on top. We may intuit that all the sections in the *Goldberg Variations* are fundamentally akin, but at the same time they appear to make an extremely rich diversity of melodies and moods, so we must seek to determine the core kinship until the solution dawns on us.

The "bass line consists of one note per measure, or thirty-two notes in total" (Petermann 2014: 152) and provides for the "numerical symmetry" of the Bach piece, whose

> thirty-two movements . . . correspond precisely to the thirty-two bars of the original theme (or the thirty-two bars in all but the few variations that demonstrate the technique of diminution, in which two bars of the theme are condensed into one bar of the variation). Additionally, the number thirty-two can be broken down into other numbers that are integral to the structure of the whole piece: twos and fours. Specifically, each movement consists of two halves, each containing sixteen measures and further reducible to four groups of four measures. (161)

This numeric symmetry is reflected in *Do Not Say We Have Nothing*, with its mathematician storyteller. The book is in two parts—part 1 and part 0—plus the "Coda." Each of the fifteen chapters (1–8 in part 1 and 7–1 in part 0, numbered in that archway order) is marked with five short horizontal lines of a music staff. There are eight chapters in part 1; chapter numbering descends from seven to one in part 0, which, together with the coda (number zero per se), makes another eight, which equals sixteen elements in total. Each but chapter 8 and the coda "occurs" twice: there are two chapters 1, two of 2, two of 3, and so on. Once we add up all the numbers, we get sixty-four. Such unity of base ("bass"), with sets of varied notes—music notes, diary notes, and the paratextual "Notes" appended at the end of the novel—and numbers easily transformable into one another, explains sympathetic family resemblances among narratorial voices (of Marie and Ai-Ming, for instance), characters (of the novel and of Chinese writing occasionally used), and event progressions in the Thien novel. Marie's story is a variation of Ai-Ming's; Sparrow can be Da-Wei of the Book of Records or Dmitri Shostakovich in Thien's references to Soviet music history; what happens to Zhuli is replayed in Kai's fate. In both chapters 1, we hear Bach's sonata for the piano and violin performed by Gould and Yehudi Menuhin (Thien 2016: 4, 447), so the cycle is complete. Like the *Goldbergs*, the novel ends before it exhausts its potential for variations.

Borges's ([1944] 1993: 66) "*Library* [of Babel] *is limitless and periodic*": once all the possible combinations of the writing symbols are used up, the universe starts all over again. The Book of Records, endlessly written on, can only register a small portion of world history, and every single event it depicts can be further expanded through the addition of more details and portrayal of more people involved. The encyclopedic aspiration to include *everything* is not denied in but signaled by the incompletion of Thien's Bach-inspired design.

Do Not Say We Have Nothing alludes to over fifty works of music—by Bach, Beethoven, Tchaikovsky, Ravel, Debussy, Mahler, Prokofiev, Shostakovich, and dozens of others, including Sparrow. Music for Sparrow, like mathematics for Marie, with its lack of "absolute claim on meaning," is the kind of freedom that "no thought could equal" (Thien 2016: 315), a way to retain an order of the self because no one can take it entirely away from you. Music connects Marie to Kai; Swirl's village teahouse singing draws Wen to her; Bach returns to Sparrow after decades of routine factory work separating him from his conservatory past, as soon as Ai-Ming and Ling give him a Walkman and a Glenn Gould *Goldberg* tape. Shortly before his death in Beijing, Sparrow, "Bird of Quiet," even goes back to composing. As Zhuli's fellow violin student, who survives the Cultural Revolution and gets readmitted to the new Shanghai Conservatory after Mao's death, remarks, "Music is nothing. It is nothing and yet it belongs to me" (Thien 2016: 303). *Do not say we have nothing*, one might paraphrase, *because we have music playing silently in our minds.*

Thien's narrative constantly balances on the verge of negativity, suffering, death, and darkness that the atrocities of the Maoist regime bring to ordinary people of various social strata—peasants and workers as well as intellectuals and party cadres. In chapter 2 of part 1, Marie cannot believe that music can be illegal, but she can feel that Sparrow's "illegal" tune, which Ai-Ming sings from memory, is filled with "grief and dignity" (35). Before the Cultural Revolution begins, Shanghai Conservatory students attack "revisionist Soviet composers" such as "the disgraced formalist" Prokofiev during sessions of public self-criticism and promise to dismiss the wrong music and replace it with the right revolutionary kind (136). But there is something that allows music to escape the brutal changes of history. Although supposedly at some point in time "the Baroque ended and Classical began" (209)—just like the age of reason canceled the Western preclassical episteme with its Chinese-style encyclopedias, in Foucault's archaeological terms—Sparrow's, and eventually Marie's, deep affection for "Old Bach" and his music "seeping through the walls" in "a tide of sadness" (74) continues across the novel. Sparrow's copy of the *Goldberg* score in "the lines and dots" of jianpu notation (84) enters the Book of (Music) Records, which is also the *"Book of Songs* and *Book of History"* (154), just like words do. There is a common denominator to everything, whereupon things cease to be untranslatable.

When Sparrow's little cousin Zhuli arrives in Shanghai after her parents' arrest, he opens the door to her for the first time and sees a tiny girl holding a vinyl record of the *Goldberg Variations*. The girl addresses him as "Bā Hè" as a matter of improvised password. But Sparrow *is* Bach, who "turned away from the linear and found his voice in the cyclical . . . God's time and in what the ancient Song and Tang scholars saw as the continual reiterations of the past" (214–15). Sparrow's symphony, which does not have a chance to finish scoring, still "exists in a different kind of space" (Lee 2019: 15)—that of another time's forking. From that space, he can hear "the Twelfth *Goldberg Variation*, two voices engaged in a slightly out-of-breath canon" in his head, played to the clinking of Beijing bicycle bells as he takes Ai-Ming to the city's architectural "zero" point, Tiananmen Square, for the first time in 1988 (Thien 2016: 358). Times and musics compress in Sparrow's mind, and the silence of his unfinished Symphony no. 3 with its unwritten fourth movement forever fills and escapes the space where he is, no worse than actual music would: "Silence too is music. Silence will last" (280).

The role that music plays in *Do Not Say We Have Nothing* supports its inherently comparative quality. Although Bach and other composers featured in the novel are associated with emphatically *Western* heritage, contrapuntal variations prompt Said's ([1993] 1994: 32) concept of a "comparative or, better, a contrapuntal perspective" cited above. Just like hearing the bass line of the polyphonic *Goldberg Variations* as its base melody must be learned, Thien's theme—every common person in history whom history strives to erase—needs to be distinguished through comparative operations of sympathetic rather than purely analytic "listening." One needs to divide contrapuntal streams into a line of alternating bits of information from each melodic part, as Thien does by alternating different characters' stories, and resynchronize them to appreciate the polyphonic unity (see Delazari 2019). By all means, there must be a *reader* to engage with such "comparative or, better, contrapuntal" outlook in the Thien novel. Otherwise, the novelistic "score" would remain unperformed.

Sympathies

At the beginning of *Do Not Say We Have Nothing*, the twenty-one-year-old Marie stops by a DVD shop in Vancouver's Chinatown to the sound of Bach's Sonata for the Piano and Violin no. 4, experiencing an unmistakably Proustian effect of involuntary memory: "And suddenly I was in the car with my father" (Thien 2016: 4). Art's capacity to let us triumph over time and space through building emotional connections with absent people and alien circumstances is well known. Associative links powered by memory are our private realizations of the comparative and contrapuntal method of treating facts that Said and Thien advocate.

Sympathies that we develop for fictional characters, whose fragmented experiences we may "enact" from a first-person stance (see Caracciolo 2014), when our embodied mind blends with them to serve as our surrogate "storyworld possible selves" (Martínez 2018), depend on the same cognitive mechanisms as those that we employ in going about our everyday lives. Thien's peculiarly encyclopedic design is, by means of creative imagination, to do away with the negativity and silence that Chinese official history imposes on people like Sparrow, Kai, and Zhuli. Once the 1989 events on Tiananmen Square, whether they are labeled as "massacre" or "protests," are censored, undermined, denied, or utterly silenced by the authorities, thousands of individuals involved in those events are canceled. Thien's "book of records" is "a counterpoint to the official history," reclaiming from oblivion "all the music, the unwritten music, all the half-finished stories, the fragmented novels, all the memories that don't get spoken aloud, all the love affairs that just dissolved" (Patterson, Polley, and Thien 2017).

The affective grip[4] that the novel seeks to take of the reader is character-

---

4. As Nancy Armstrong (2014) demonstrates, contemporary novels do not need to rely on readerly sympathies to maintain that affective grip, since even characters who fail to overcome their "third-personhood" and thus prevent us from identifying with them appeal strongly to our "primordial selves" of preconceptual bodily responses. Thien does not go that far, but among novels that are thematically related to hers and published after Armstrong's "Affective Turn" article, Adam Johnson's North Korean fantasy *The Orphan Master's Son* (2016) comes to mind naturally to supplement Armstrong's example set.

istic of other contemporary encyclopedic fictions, which are—somewhat surprisingly—reader friendly (see Kyllönen 2018: 34–35, 41–42). In addition, the genre's "ethical commitment" is often realized through "maximalist themes" (Ercolino 2012: 252) rotating around great historical traumas.

Readerly sympathy cannot be taken for granted, though, as there may be obstacles in its way. In assessing the interrelational narrative webs of "big, ambitious novels," Wood (2000) finds "something essentially paranoid about the belief that everything is connected to everything else," which such narratives express. He also complains about "hysterical" realism's absence of convincing characters and its consequent failure to engage readers emotionally. When asked if she intends her book for mainland Chinese readers, whose attitude to her subject matters may be rather complicated, Thien says, "Yes. I think a lot about what it would feel like to pick up a book like mine and feel that your life and history has been misrepresented, has been made superficial or has been skewed into something else—that is what I really don't want" (Lee 2019: 16).

Unlike my Russian 2019 undergraduate literature majors in St. Petersburg, some of my comparative literature MA students in Hong Kong the year before, to whom the novel was assigned for an elective twenty-first-century fiction course, proved to be strongly resistant to *Do Not Say We Have Nothing*. Faults were found with Thien's errors in Chinese as well as her unlikely situations and unconvincing characters. There seemed to be a consensus among several students, for example, that such a freethinking character as Big Mother Knife and especially her conduct with her husband were totally against the odds. Most importantly, however, the suppressed irritation with—even resentment at—the novel was backed with the argument that Thien did not know what she was writing about: born a Canadian citizen, she had not witnessed any of the history that her book dramatizes. Even the music determining the author's axiological and aesthetic posture is all but Western and so is her overall ideology. Therefore, Thien hardly has the right to speak about such things. Questionable reliability due to improper personal, national, and cultural background disqualifies the novelist despite her authentic ethnicity and illegitimatizes the narrative for some readers: while the events in *Do Not Say We Have Nothing* are "ontologically" possible (see Ryan 2019: 66), its affective outreach may fail against a *national* experiential background (the students in question came from mainland China). Most Russian students read *Do Not Say We Have Nothing* as simply a "Chinese novel," or even a source of information about China, with plenty of meaningful allusions and parallels to Soviet history. Some mainland Chinese readers, conversely, found the book emphatically *non*-Chinese, experiencing it as deeply alien, even painfully alienating. Thien's attempt at communicating the recent tragedies of her ancestral land to the world in order to "implicate all of us" in a contrapuntal comparison, since "their history is our history" (Lee 2019: 16), may thus not be universally successful.

It proved to be difficult to reverse those students' negative attitudes by arguing that *Do Not Say We Have Nothing* was a work of fiction, not history, and was therefore not committed to factual precision, so all kinds of improbable characters could inhabit its diegetic premises. The author's alibi of what Boris Tomashevsky (1965) called *realistic motivation*—namely, the fact that Thien's narrator, Marie, is also a Canadian with limited Chinese—did not impress the students, either. The reader's decision of whether to sympathize with a book or not is fundamentally preconceptual: the storyworld just *feels* wrong to some readers and right to others. However, a favorable or unfavorable impression is a process rather than a given, and it has much to do with the reader's continuous judgment on "vraisemblance." In Karin Kukkonen's (2017: 25) "Bayesian" model of how eighteenth-century English novels work cognitively, "not only do readers prefigure what should happen to people with particular characteristics and how characters should act in a particular set of circumstances, as decorum suggests; instead, the entire process of narrative can be understood as movement through revisions of probabilities." In the late Hayden White's similarly Aristotelian view, once we are interested less in "facts" (what happened?) than in the conditions that made those facts possible, we enter the realm of "literary art understood as a mode of cognition focused on the possible, rather than on the actual (history, as Aristotle understood it) and the universal (philosophy, as he understood it)" (White 2014: 34). Leaning on speech act theory, White insists that all utterances—historiographic, philosophical, and literary—are actions meant to "change the world"; their factuality may thus be well less important than their significance for human practices (39).

In a sense, Thien's "Chinese encyclopedia" approach negates statistical probability, since life under totalitarian rule is predictably unpredictable, hence the flexibility and variability of plot in the Book of Records. The book escapes from means of official control through its parabolic treatment of characters, multiple encodings, collective authorship, and forking courses of adventures. Marie is indeed very marginal in the tale about twentieth-century Chinese trauma best represented by Sparrow and his extended family. She finds herself in the position of Melville's Ishmael—as the only person left to tell since other witnesses are all dead or gone. In addition, she is also profoundly engaged with that story because it can help her resolve a personal matter: mourn her parents. Understanding the "situational logic" at the core of *Do Not Say We Have Nothing* as one of those texts that "carry their own reading instructions within them" is, by analogy with Kukkonen's (2017: 219) neoclassical material, the way "to fully engage with it." Readers are entitled to rebel and refuse to play by Thien's rules, but it is their choice, not the novel's immanent property.

Thien's invitation is for the reader to look into "the shadow part of history," listen to the "inside silences," play "the unwritten music," and discover its "lost musicians—things that couldn't come into being but maybe there was still a shadow of them" (Lee 2019: 14). *Do Not Say We Have Nothing* is a novelistic "Chinese encyclopedia" of things real and implausible, which can be retraced to a forking in world history by means of what White (2014: 5) calls "imaginative hypothetization." It is not about the historical past, which obeys the rigors of historiography in its selective acknowledgment of only those past things that display their material traces (*documents*) at present. Thien is after the alternative "practical past" unaccounted for by historians—one "that people as individuals or members of groups draw upon in order to help them make assessments and make decisions" (White 2014: xiii). It is "a past which . . . serves as the basis for the kinds of perceptions of situations, solutions of problems, and judgments of value and worth that we must make in everyday situations of the kind never experienced by the 'heroes' of history" (14–15). Novelists from Walter Scott and Jane Austen to W. G. Sebald and Toni Morrison bring precisely this kind of past to life in writing about "the present *as* history" (13). People's thoughts and feelings, banned from historical discourse unless properly documented, are of paramount value, and it is through novelistic invention, which is also a practical action, that such crucial content of history becomes available to us. Thien's (and Marie's) narration about violence and suffering in China is, in extension of White's argument, not as much about what people did under the circumstances as about what *she*—Madeleine Thien, Jiang Li-Ling—or *we* would do if all that happened to us. Thien is responsible for just the same as what White credits Morrison for in *Beloved* (1987)—namely, "for inventing the thoughts of her protagonist[s] . . . and, in so doing, claiming her freedom to deal with the past in a way consonant with her situation in her present" (White 2014: 23–24). Constant reminders in the text that we are dealing with "a copy of a copy" are not disclaimers but articulations of a normal state of literary affairs.

White's (2014: 45) other useful distinction is between events, which happen, and facts, which are "established" by historians, described, and attributed a "proper" name. Events, including those that constitute "big" facts—the Russian Revolution of 1917 or the Renaissance (46)—may become factualized. When Thien deals with such big facts as the Cultural Revolution, she splits them back into events. Through fictional characters, she rebuilds the experiential dimension that those events necessarily lose in being established as facts. Unlike the account of the Tiananmen Square protests in an encyclopedia, which must conventionally stick to facts, Thien *fictionalizes* facts by creating characters and their internal monologues. The novel liberates facts from the confines of history, with its "feeling of inevitability": "History knows how things are going to turn out, but for individuals, nothing is inevitable" (Lee 2019: 14). As Mikhail Bakhtin ([1963] 1984: 59) puts it in his treatment of characters in Fyodor Dostoevsky's "polyphonic" novels, "As long as a person is alive he lives by the fact that he is not yet finalized." Said ([1993] 1994: 31–32) warns us against overlooking such "unfinalized" quality in comparative studies:

> If you know in advance that the African or Iranian or Chinese or Jewish or German experience is fundamentally integral, coherent, separate, and therefore comprehensible only to Africans, Iranians, Chinese, Jews, or Germans, you first of all posit as essential something which . . . is both historically created and the result of interpretation—namely the existence of Africanness, Jewishness, or Germanness, or for that matter Orientalism and Occidentalism. And second, you are likely as a consequence to defend the essence or experience itself rather than promote full knowledge of it and its entanglements and dependencies on other knowledges.

By its refusal to treat events, facts, and people as fossils, *Do Not Say We Have Nothing* maintains a different, inherently comparative focus on the Chinese experience.

In Rita Felski's (2015: 2) estimation, the general "spirit of skeptical questioning or outright condemnation" has dominated literary and cultural studies after the New Criticism, maintaining a variety of forms in different schools of thought. More recently, old charges of the affective fallacy have been partially dismissed in the gradual spread of cognitive approaches to literature, suggesting that "critique is as much a matter of affect and rhetoric as of philosophy or politics" and aiming "to de-essentialize the practice of suspicious reading" (3). One can learn from a "big, ambitious," and, arguably, encyclopedic novel such as Thien's instead of striving to catch the author by the hand whenever she contradicts herself or betrays the reader's sense of realism. Such learning implies attending to the inherently comparative "reading instructions" within the novel itself (Kuk-konen 2017: 219) while staying "on the same plane" with it instead of "casting around for a hidden puppeteer who is pulling the strings" (Felski 2015: 6), in a "paranoid reading" estimation (see Sedgwick 1997). Although such novels may seem overloaded with facts and/or lacking verisimilitude, they "contain multi-tudes," in Walt Whitman's idiom, and thus help less suspicious readers build new connections and compare things across nationalisms and regional novelistic cultures, Western or Eastern, beyond their own (hence Said's plural "knowledges").

As the author declares in an interview, *Do Not Say We Have Nothing* "is sometimes thought of as a novel that's critical towards China. I actually don't agree. This novel has been a labour of love" (Patterson, Polley, and Thien 2017). But instead of "looking behind the text—for its hidden causes, determin-ing conditions, and noxious motives" or the author's biographical and cultural background—"we might place ourselves in front of the text, reflecting on what it unfurls, calls forth, makes possible" and recognizing it as our "coactor" (Felski 2015: 12). Thien's novel, with its inherently comparative capacities, rescues us from a vicious circularity. Where the critique of literature reads literature as cri-tique, Thien's novel, from its title on, denies the denial and seeks to save, affirm, and reconnect. What it offers the reader is indeed "new forms of identification, subjectivity, and perceptual possibility" (Felski 2015: 17). Marie, on her part, is not critical of what people tell her about Sparrow, Zhuli, and Kai in Vancouver, Hong Kong, and Shanghai. She is sympathetic because now she is aware of how facts are made and events unmade: those who let Ai-Ming and her mother collect what may or may not be Sparrow's ashes tell Ling that her husband died of "a stroke," "at home" (Thien 2016: 448).

Do Not Say We Have Nothing affords various reading biases—postmodern, intermedial, postcolonial, metahistorical, cognitive, or postcritical. This article originated in my experience of teaching the novel for two subsequent years to three different audiences and the impulse to explain a hostile response to the novel, which puzzled me so much back in Hong Kong. It is not that anyone has ever asked me to be Thien's advocate—nor does she need such advocacy, as the novel speaks effectively for itself. There were also students in both Hong Kong and St. Petersburg who loved the novel, and together with others who did not, they had brilliant insights about the book's messages. As an inherently comparative text, *Do Not Say We Have Nothing* provides room for all.

When Ai-Ming listens to Wen the Dreamer and Swirl's stories in Dunhuang, before crossing the Chinese western border to avoid the danger of post-Tiananmen prosecution in 1990, she cries "even when the story was a happy one" and, "when the story was sad," feels "nothing, not even the beating of her own heart" (Thien 2016: 457). Like the zeros and silences of the novel, this emotional numbness is *not* "nothing"—in fact, it is everything insofar as it is a fragment of an infinite chain of affects, which resists a finalizing judgment: when Foucault laughs at Borges's "Chinese encyclopedia," he takes it very seriously nonetheless.

Do Not Say We Have Nothing may be useless as an encyclopedia per se: one may pick a different reference source on Chinese history at any time to find conceptual information, each fact properly established and appended with dates and contexts that distinguish it from its infinite others. The novel is not to be read for facts—only for events and feelings before they are devoured by oblivious historical past. Events may be fictitious, but the sympathies and antipathies of reading are real.

White (2014: x) cites an old teacher of his saying that "history is the story of communities . . . defining themselves as opposed to their others, when in reality there are only differences among them." East and West are not contrasted in *Do Not Say We Have Nothing*—just present in myriad connections and continuities, as well as separations and differences. When Said defined comparative literature as "a field whose origin and purpose is to move beyond insularity and provincialism and to see several cultures and literatures together, contrapuntally" (Said [1993] 1994: 43), he might just as well have been talking about Thien's book.

Ivan Delazari is associate professor of philology at HSE University in St. Petersburg. He is author of *Musical Stimulacra: Literary Narrative and the Urge to Listen* (2021).

Works Cited

Armstrong, Nancy. 2014. "The Affective Turn in Contemporary Fiction." *Contemporary Literature* 55, no. 3: 441–65.

Bakhtin, Mikhail. (1963) 1984. *Problems of Dostoevsky's Poetics*. Translated by Caryl Emerson. Minneapolis: University of Minnesota Press.

Belinsky, V. G. 1974. *Izbranniye stat'i (Selected Articles)*. Saratov, USSR: Privolzhskoe knizhnoe izdatel'stvo.

Boddy, Kasia. 2019. "Making It Long: Men, Women, and the Great American Novel Now." *Textual Practice* 33, no. 2: 318–37.

Borges, Jorge Luis. (1944) 1993. *Ficciones.* Translated by Anthony Kerrigan, Helen Temple, and Ruthven Todd. New York: Knopf.

Borges, Jorge Luis. (1964) 1975. *Other Inquisitions, 1937–1952.* Translated by Ruth L. C. Simms. Austin: University of Texas Press.

Caracciolo, Marco. 2014. *The Experientiality of Narrative: An Enactivist Approach.* Berlin: de Gruyter.

Caracciolo, Marco. 2019. "Ungrounding Fictional Worlds: An Enactivist Perspective on the 'Worldlikeness' of Fiction." In *Possible Worlds Theory and Contemporary Narratology*, edited by Alice Bell and Marie-Laure Ryan, 113–31. Lincoln: University of Nebraska Press.

Delazari, Ivan. 2019. "Contrafactual Counterpoint: Revisiting the Polyphonic Novel Metaphor with Faulkner's *The Wild Palms.*" *CounterText* 5, no. 3: 371–94.

Delazari, Ivan. 2021. *Musical Stimulacra: Literary Narrative and the Urge to Listen.* New York: Routledge.

Ercolino, Stefano. 2012. "The Maximalist Novel." *Comparative Literature* 64, no. 3: 241–56.

Felski, Rita. 2015. *The Limits of Critique.* Chicago: University of Chicago Press.

Foucault, Michel. (1966) 1994. *The Order of Things: An Archaeology of the Human Sciences.* New York: Vintage.

Goethe, Johann Wolfgang von. (1906) 1984. *Conversations with Eckermann, 1823–1832.* Translated by John Oxenford. San Francisco: North Point.

Karl, Frederick R. 1985. "American Fictions: The Mega-Novel." *Conjunctions*, no. 7: 248–60.

Kukkonen, Karin. 2017. *A Prehistory of Cognitive Poetics: Neoclassicism and the Novel.* New York: Oxford University Press.

Kyllönen, Vesa. 2018. "Information and the Illusion of Totality: Reading the Contemporary Encyclopedic Novel." In *Reading Today*, edited by Arnoldo Hax and Lionel Olavarría, 31–44. London: UCL Press.

LeClair, Tom. 1987. *In the Loop: Don DeLillo and the Systems Novel.* Urbana: University of Illinois Press.

Lee, Hsiu-chuan. 2019. "Writing, History, and Music in *Do Not Say We Have Nothing*: A Conversation with Madeleine Thien." *Canadian Literature*, no. 238: 13–28.

Letzler, David. 2017. *The Cruft of Fiction: Mega-Novels and the Science of Paying Attention.* Lincoln: University of Nebraska Press.

Martínez, María-Ángeles. 2018. *Storyworld Possible Selves.* Berlin: de Gruyter.

Mendelson, Edward. 1976. "Encyclopedic Narrative: From Dante to Pynchon." *MLN* 91, no. 6: 1267–75.

Moretti, Franco. 2013. *Distant Reading.* London: Verso.

Patterson, Christopher B., Jason S. Polley, and Madeleine Thien. 2017. "Beneath the Slogans: Interview with Madeleine Thien on *Do Not Say We Have Nothing* (2017)." *Cha*, no. 38. www.asiancha.com/content/view/2931/651/.

Petermann, Emily. 2014. *The Musical Novel: Imitation of Musical Structure, Performance, and Reception in Contemporary Fiction*. Rochester, NY: Camden House.

Ryan, Marie-Laure. 2019. "From Possible Worlds to Storyworlds: On the Worldness of Narrative Representation." In *Possible Worlds Theory and Contemporary Narratology*, edited by Alice Bell and Marie-Laure Ryan, 62–87. Lincoln: University of Nebraska Press.

Said, Edward W. (1993) 1994. *Culture and Imperialism*. New York: Vintage.

Sedgwick, Eve Kosofsky. 1997. "Paranoid Reading and Reparative Reading; or, You're So Paranoid, You Probably Think This Introduction Is about You." In *Novel Gazing: Queer Readings in Fiction*, edited by Eve Kosofsky Sedgwick, 1–38. Durham, NC: Duke University Press.

Thien, Madeleine. 2016. *Do Not Say We Have Nothing*. New York: Norton.

Tomashevsky, Boris. 1965. "Thematics." In *Russian Formalist Criticism: Four Essays*, translated by Lee T. Lemon and Marion J. Reis, 62–95. Lincoln: University of Nebraska Press.

White, Hayden. 2014. *The Practical Past*. Evanston, IL: Northwestern University Press.

Wood, James. 2000. "Human, All Too Inhuman: On the Formation of a New Genre; Hysterical Realism." *New Republic*, July 24. newrepublic.com/article/61361/human-inhuman.

The Structure of Scares:
Art, Horror, and Immersion in Marisha Pessl's
Night Film

MELISSA C. MACERO

The narrator of Marisha Pessl's novel *Night Film* (2014a: 165) likens watching one of (fictional) horror director Stanislas Cordova's films to entering a new, darker reality: "To watch the film *once* was to be lost in so many graphic, edge-of-your-seat scenes, that when it was over, I remembered feeling vaguely astounded that I'd returned to the real world. Something about the film's darkness made me wonder if I *would*." The narrator, investigative journalist Scott McGarth, is so engrossed in Cordova's films that the "real world" disappears, being replaced by the horror at the heart of the films. Pessl's novel strives to create a similar effect through its formal use of multimodal elements, such as reproduced web pages, emails, text messages, photographs, news articles, and police reports that pepper its almost six hundred pages. These artifacts use everyday ephemera to lure the reader into Cordova's world and to frame this world as one that looks almost exactly like ours but isn't quite. The ambition, then, of Pessl's novel—and Cordova's films—is to solicit an almost complete immersion of the reader (or viewer) into the story at hand. While this ambition is, in certain aspects, obviously an impossible one, it is also an ambition that is central to the two main genres the novel engages with: horror and what Stefano Ercolino (2015) calls the "maximalist novel."

The horror genre in particular requires a certain level of immersion in order to be successful. For horror, as Noël Carroll (1990: 8) and its name suggest, is "designed to produce an emotional effect." At first glance, then, it would appear as though the response of the reader (or viewer) to a given text would be the

Genre, Vol. 54, No. 2   July 2021
DOI 10.1215/00166928-9263091   © 2021 by University of Oklahoma

determining factor in its success as a work of horror. The reader is either scared and therefore the right emotional effect is produced, or she's not, and the text is a failure. As we shall see, though, this emotional immersion central to the genre is not as straightforward as it first appears. Moreover, if the sole aim of horror is to solicit engagement from its audience, then works of horror would have no meaning beyond that engagement. In other words, the parameters of what makes a "good" horror novel or film would merely be whether the majority of the audience is scared. The scares themselves, then, would supersede any interest in the form or structure of the text or film, as all that would matter is the audience's reaction, thus turning horror into merely a factory of scares.[1] I will argue, however, that horror, and more specifically novels such as *Night Film*, are more than just scare factories and can be self-legislating works whose success or failure is determined by internal, as opposed to external, factors.[2]

In this respect, although the most spectacular and apparently defining feature of the genre is the effect it seeks to produce on the audience, a novel like *Night Film* actually embodies something like what Theodor Adorno ([1970] 1997: 226) called the effort to structure itself not in terms of its relation to that audience but "according to its own immanent law." This internal structuring allows the work to exist in opposition to that audience and society more generally and is the founda-

---

1. See, for example, the recent Forbes article, "What Is the Scariest Movie Ever? Science Now Has an Answer to That Question" (Bean 2020), which summarizes a "scientific study" that used average audience heart rates to rate the "scariness" of horror films. One of the many issues with this study is that it focuses solely on jump-scares and any consequent rises in beats per minute of the audience, thereby limiting the parameters of "scariness" to purely physical reactions, downplaying or even outright ignoring the more psychological effects of dread, uneasiness, and anxiety that can linger long after the credits roll. And so, regardless of whether or not the audience understands what is happening in the film as well as how well (or poorly) the film itself is constructed, all that matters here is its ability to catch the audience off guard.

2. A version of this claim is also central to the study of the relatively new subgenre of "posthorror" that arose right around the same time as *Night Film*'s publication (2013–2014) and includes films such as *It Follows* (2014), *Get Out* (2017), *Hereditary* (2018), and *A Quiet Place* (2018). As David Church (2021: 2) notes in his recently published book on this rising mode, *Post-horror: Art, Genre, and Cultural Elevation*, posthorror is seen as a "major site of both artistic innovation and cultural distinction" within the larger horror genre. Posthorror, also called "elevated horror" or "smart horror," is largely understood by film critics to mark more "artistic" horror films that prioritize atmosphere, social commentary, and style over formulaic jump-scares and monsters. Church, on the other hand, shies away from such hierarchization and instead argues that posthorror is "far more accurately described as an aesthetically linked *cycle* within the longer and broader tradition of art-horror cinema" (3), which dates back to the modernist films of the 1930s. Therefore, instead of reading posthorror as an attempt to move beyond the constraints of the horror genre, Church argues that it is instead a reimagining of a particular style of horror film. Similarly to Church, then, my argument here is less concerned with valorizing a certain kind of horror over another and instead seeks to highlight how Pessl mobilizes the genre and its perceived hierarchies within her novel.

tion of what Adorno calls "artistic autonomy." *Night Film* not only distances itself from its audience but also identifies this appeal to the audience with what Pessl understands as a gendering of the male-centered horror movie and by imagining its alternative—the horror novel—as in some crucial sense female. The masculinization of the sort of visceral response demanded by horror films is embodied in the narrator, Scott McGarth, and his complete immersion into the mystery surrounding Cordova's daughter. The form and structure of *Night Film*, as we shall see, complicates McGarth's narration and immersion in seeking an alternative.

We must first examine, though, the role of the reader in determining the immersiveness of a novel and defining the concept of immersion itself. And so, three accounts of immersion will be integral to our understanding of how the term functions in *Night Film*, as well as horror and the maximalist novel. The most explicit difference between these accounts is the level of involvement they each ascribe to the reader and her responses in describing how immersion is achieved within a literary work. Marie-Laure Ryan argues that the reader is the central component in determining the immersiveness of a text. Noël Carroll, however, asserts that the text itself determines what is the appropriate response of the reader through "art-horror." Lastly, Stefano Ercolino, although not preoccupied with how the reader responds, nonetheless insists that part of what makes the central aspects of the maximalist novel—length, encyclopedism, and so on—so important is how they facilitate the level of readerly engagement required to get through a lengthy novel.

Due to her focus on the reader, Ryan (2015: 9) defines immersion as "the experience through which a fictional world acquires the presence of an autonomous, language-independent reality populated with live human beings." The world of the text, therefore, becomes almost as—if not just as—real as the world around us. This is a "corporeal experience" (13), which "presupposes an imaginative relationship to a *world projected by text*" (9). In other words, immersion for Ryan is the bodily and emotional response of a reader to a text and more specifically to the world and characters being presented within that text. This response, moreover, is dependent upon the process of "recentering," during which the reader's "consciousness relocates itself to another world and . . . recognizes the entire universe of being around this virtual reality" (73). Through this process, the world of the text becomes "actual" (73) and the reader can virtually inhabit it much as she physically inhabits her own world.

Successful immersion, therefore, "takes the projection of a virtual body . . .

to feel integrated in an art world" (13). This projected body is incorporated into the text by the reader herself, and its ability to interact with the textual world is dependent upon the engagement of that reader. As Ryan notes, "The degree of precision and the nature of the immersed reader's mental representation depend in part on her individual disposition, in part on whether the focus of attention is character, plot, or setting" (85). The precise form of a reader's immersion is dependent upon both the text itself—its formal aspects, such as point of view, tense, voice, and so on, as well as its content character types, such as real or imagined locations, types of events, and so on—and, more importantly, the response of the reader to these aspects of the text, a response governed by her "individual disposition." Thus, while the text itself would not change from one reader to the next, the response of each reader would change, and so, according to Ryan, would the immersiveness of the text.

Carroll, on the other hand, argues that the subjective responses of a reader should be irrelevant to our understanding of the emotional immersiveness of a text, and, more specifically, of a horror text. Such texts are designed to produce an emotional effect called "art-horror," as opposed to "natural horror," such as what we may feel in response to particularly gruesome or terrifying real-world events.[3] Art-horror, however, can only be solicited by the "characteristic structures, imagery, and figures" of the genre and how they are arranged in specific works (Carroll 1990: 8). Therefore, although art-horror is an emotion, it is not located outside of the work but rather is immanent to the work itself. As Carroll notes:

> Rather than characterizing art-horror solely on the basis of our own subjective responses, we can ground our conjectures on observations of the way in which characters respond to the monsters in works of horror. That is, if we proceed under the assumption that our emotional responses as audience members are supposed to parallel those of characters in important respects, then we can begin to portray horror by noting the emotional features that authors and directors attribute to characters molested by monsters. (18–19)

In Carroll's framework, art-horror is an objective feature of a given work, which is largely constructed through emotional content. The actions and emotions of the characters offer a blueprint for how the reader should respond, and that response

---

3. Carroll's use of the term *art-horror* is also very different from that of scholars such as Joan Hawkins (2000), who use it to delineate a specific stylistic mode within the genre. As David Church (2021: 8) succinctly describes it, this kind of art-horror is "far less an evaluative modification of the genre label than a much more literal means of evoking the combination of *art cinema* as a formally distinctive mode of film practice and the *horror genre* as an established set of storytelling conventions, iconography, and themes."

is art-horror. Art-horror, then, is a normative form of immersion in that it is prescribed by the text itself and should not vary from one reader to the next.

Thus, whether or not the audience *is* art-horrified is unimportant to Carroll's theory and to the art-horror of the works themselves:

> I am not preoccupied with the actual relations of works of art-horror to audiences, but with a normative relation, the response the audience is supposed to have to the work of art-horror. I believe that we are able to get at this by presuming that the work of art-horror has built into it, so to speak, a set of instructions about the appropriate way the audience is supposed to respond to it. . . . Works of horror, that is, teach us, in large measure, the appropriate way to respond to them. Unearthing those cues or instructions is an empirical matter, not an exercise in subjective projection. (31)

Horror, according to Carroll, offers an emotional road map to its readers through the various responses of the characters, and whether a reader decides to follow that map or not is beyond the scope of the art-horror of the text. While almost every genre of fiction that includes human or anthropomorphized characters offers emotional guidance to its readers in that the affective responses produced by the text are usually also presented in it (for the most part, we laugh and cry with the characters, as opposed to at them), the horror genre adds another layer to this situation in that the reader is asked to respond to events and characters that not only are not real but also could never be real.

As Carroll states, "We want to know how it is that we can be horrified by fictions—by beings and events that, in some sense, do not exist and which we must know do not exist, if we are to be art-horrified" (59). In other words, how could the reader ever truly parallel the responses of the characters when they are faced with a creature that she herself could never meet and that she knows is unreal? Are readers engaging in a sort of make-believe experience where they are simply pretending to be scared? Carroll's answer to this quandary is what he calls the "thought theory of emotional responses to fictions" (79). In the thought theory, "We are not pretending to be horrified; we are genuinely horrified, but by the thought of Dracula rather than by our conviction that we are his next victim" (86). To rephrase, it is not Dracula, the character, that scares the reader but the thought of Dracula and his fellow vampires that horrifies her, or more precisely that should horrify her.

Similarly to Carroll's analysis of art-horror, Ercolino is primarily interested in immersive attributes that are intrinsic to the text itself, as opposed to those that are external to it. Whereas for Carroll art-horror is a thematic instruction manual, for Ercolino the defining aspect of a maximalist novel is structural:

namely, length. The maximalist novel is above all long, and this lengthiness is a "possibility tied to the strongly innovative and experimental nature of maximalist novels as well as to their epic, totalizing ambition" (Ercolino 2015: 19).[4] It is through this extension of length, then, that these novels are able to produce an "epic" text that lures the reader in and can, therefore, justify its literal and figurative weight. Lengthiness is the scaffolding upon which the maximalist novelist is able to construct a complete world for the reader to inhabit: "A text that aspires to rival the entire world cannot do so except by assuming the latter's amplitude" (21). Moreover, the attributes necessary to build the world of the maximalist novel "would not, in a restricted space, be able to fully express their potential as 'world effects'" (21). In other words, the multiplicity of pages offers the requisite space in which to employ the other primary attributes of the maximalist novel that are necessary to the dynamism of the textual world.

One such attribute, the paranoid imagination, is the core of the maximalist novel, as it is the mechanism through which the "world effects" made possible via the length are connected. This paranoia is "the *motor* of the maximalist literary imagination" (106) in that "everything is linked: this is the unshakeable conviction of the paranoid, a conviction that finds its structural equivalent in the direct or indirect interconnection of all the stories, of all of the characters, and of all the events that proliferate in maximalist novels" (111). In other words, it is this sense of eventual cohesion—that everything will come together in the end because all of the events and characters are connected in some way—that propels the narrative forward and thereby compels the reader to commit to a literary journey of hundreds of pages. This paranoid imagination is a "veritable *holistic ontology* [that] seems to take shape because of which no event can be either conceived or fully comprehended if not within a much more far-reaching design" (111). Every aspect of a maximalist novel is a part of the whole of the narrative, and so that narrative could not be complete without each of them. This promise of a whole is what allows the world of a maximalist novel to become a complete alternative reality. The ontological status of paranoia in the maximalist novel, then, is structurally similar to that of Carroll's art-horror in that it is immanent to the work itself and independent of any actual paranoia on the part of the reader.

---

4. He identifies ten aspects central to the maximalist novel, which are (in the order presented by Ercolino): length, encyclopedic mode, dissonant chorality, diegetic exuberance, completeness, narratorial omniscience, paranoid imagination, intersemioticity, ethical commitment, and hybrid realism (Ercolino 2015: xiii–xiv).

Paranoia alone, however, will not facilitate the creation of a multidimensional world, according to Ercolino. Rather, this paranoid imagination must be complemented by the "encyclopedic mode." This mode is a "particular aesthetic and cognitive attitude, consisting of a more or less heightened and totalizing narrative tension in the synthetic representation of heterogenous realities and domains of knowledge" (Ercolino 2015: 39). To rephrase, the encyclopedic mode is what allows the maximalist novel to construct a multifaceted and dynamic world that is not restricted to a single subject position (or even to multiple homogenous subject positions) but is instead heterogenous and therefore total. The "goal" of this mode is to create a "synthetic representation of the *totality* of the real" (31). This "totality of the real" that is the ultimate aim of the maximalist novel, then, is a form of the type of inhabitable textual world discussed by Ryan. Whereas for Ryan the type of immersive relationship required between reader and text is literal, for Ercolino this immersion is merely a representation in that while a readerly presence is acknowledged by the structure of the text itself, it is not required by it. In other words, the maximalist novel does not depend upon the actual engagement of the reader in order to be an immersive totality; rather, it is a totality that is constructed only to be read, as opposed to inhabited. This representational immersion is also central to Carroll's art-horror, despite the vehicle for the representation being more thematic—the situations and emotions of the characters—than structural. The ultimate level of involvement by a particular reader, or set of readers, therefore, is immaterial to both the totalizing ambition as well as the art-horror of a novel.

This distinction between a literal and a represented textual immersion of the reader is at the heart of Pessl's *Night Film* in that it is both depicted in and demanded by the novel itself. As we have seen, the narrator, Scott McGarth, has a Ryan-esque literal engagement with Cordova's films in that he—and the other viewers he witnesses and imagines—becomes completely "lost" in the films. This type of immersion is subsequently reproduced in his narration and thereby the structure of the novel. Most notably, it is produced via the novel's multimodal frame, which is established through the opening chapter that consists entirely of reproduced web pages, including a *New York Times* obituary (fig. 1). These pages are as fictional as the novel itself and yet are completely realistic representations. These web pages serve a dual function in that they provide expositional details to the reader—Cordova's daughter has allegedly committed suicide—and they establish a tangible connection between the world of the text and the world of the reader—the *New York Times* would indeed cover such a tragedy. We, the read-

http://www.nytimes.com/2011/10/14/ashley-cordova-24-found-dead

HOME PAGE | TODAY'S PAPER | VIDEO | MOST POPULAR

Log In | Register Now | Help

The New York Times

N.Y. / Region

Search All NYTimes.com

Go

WORLD | U.S. | N.Y. / REGION | BUSINESS | TECHNOLOGY | SCIENCE | HEALTH | SPORTS | OPINION | ARTS | STYLE

Ashley Cordova, 24, Found Dead

Ashley Cordova, 24, Found Dead
Published: October 14, 2011 by Charles Dunbar

Photograph courtesy of K&M Recording

A body that was found in a vacant Chinatown warehouse Thursday was identified by the city medical examiner as that of Ashley Cordova, daughter of the Academy-Award-winning American film director Stanislas Cordova. She was 24.

The cause of death has not yet been determined, but the police are investigating reports that Ms. Cordova, who reportedly had a history of depression, committed suicide by jumping into an out-of-service elevator shaft, said Hector J. Marcos, the chief spokesman for the city medical examiner's office.

Ms. Cordova was a classical pianist and former child prodigy. She made her Carnegie Hall debut at age 12, playing Ravel's Piano Concerto in G Major with the Moscow Philharmonic Orchestra. Ms. Cordova retreated from music at age 14, declining further recitals, tours and public appearances.

She was raised at The Peak, her father's vast, private Adirondack estate, which served as the setting for many of Mr. Cordova's films, including his 1979 psychological thriller, "Thumbscrew." Ms. Cordova graduated from Amherst College in 2009. Unlike her half-brother, Theo Cordova, who frequently acted in his father's films, Ms. Cordova appeared only once, playing the youngest of the Stevens children in "To Breathe with Kings" (1996), adapted from the novel by August Hauer.

The Cordova family could not be reached for comment.

Figure 1. Opening web page of Marisha Pessl's *Night Film* (2014a).
This image is a scan of the book itself.

ers, view these web pages along with McGarth, following the expositional pieces from page to page, constructing a narrative. He clicks through from news story to news story, and we see the URL at the top of the site change and the scroll bar on the side change length with each page's respective word count. We are reading over McGarth's shoulder and therefore enter into the mysterious world of the Cordova family along with him.

And yet, despite our identification with McGarth, there remains an unbridgeable gap between the reader and these web pages. We may be able to follow him down the Cordova rabbit hole, but we are unable to click and scroll like he can. For the reader, these web pages are not code to interact with, but paper and ink. We can see the scroll bar on the right-hand side of the screen but can't scroll down. We watch the URLs change from page to page but are unable to enter one of our own. And so, while McGarth's literal immersion in this mystery is being depicted, the type of immersion demanded by the novel itself is more in line with that outlined by Ercolino and Carroll. The literal immersion of the reader is not only unnecessary to the text but also prohibited by it. We can never be as engaged as McGarth because no matter how much detail is included, from the scroll bar to the deceptively realistic URLs, we can only read the content and flip the page.

This conflict between the reader's thematic and literal encounter with these web pages introduces us to the novel's intricate staging of the question of immersion. As we have seen, Cordova's films solicit such an extreme level of engagement from the viewer that she becomes "lost" in the films and is surprised to be able to return to the "real world" when the credits roll. The "graphic, edge-of-your-seat" horror of these films draws the viewer in so completely that the world of the film becomes the only one that matters. Moreover, the darkness of these films seeps into the world of the viewer, casting a shadow over reality. As McGarth explains, "I remembered feeling vaguely astounded that I'd returned to the real world. Something about the film's darkness made me wonder if I *would*—as if witnessing such things I was irrevocably breaking myself in (*or just breaking myself*), arriving at an understanding about humanity so dark, so deep down inside my own soul, I could never go back to the way I was before" (Pessl 2014a: 165). Cordova's films, then, are such a "corporeal experience"—to borrow from Ryan—that the viewer is forever changed.

Again, though, there is a disconnect between the type of immersion being described in the novel and that elicited by it. For no matter how detailed a sum-mary or how many stills are included, the reader has not and can never watch these films. They exist only in the pages of the novel and are therefore inaccessible in their true filmic form to the reader. And so the novel urges us to reevaluate the terms we have been discussing thus far. Whereas for the theoretical accounts of immersion we've examined a literal form of immersion as described by Ryan depends upon the reader's experience of the text at hand and their ability to virtually enter into it, and the representational form of immersion as put forth by Carroll and Ercolino is fully dependent upon the thematic and structural devices located within the text itself, Pessl inverts the immersive implications of these terms. The novel presents itself thematically and structurally as a thoroughly immersive text built to invite the reader into its pages. The literal involvement of the reader, though, is foreclosed by her inability to participate in a central aspect of this world: watching one of Cordova's films. *Night Film*, then, depicts the ability to become immersed in this world through both McGarth and the multimodal elements we investigate along with him, while simultaneously distancing the reader from the journalist and these elements. We cannot interact with the web pages, emails, and films of Cordova's world in their true forms of strings of code and reels of film because we are blocked by ink and paper.

At the same time, however, the reader was able to quite literally interact with this world beyond the novel's pages when the book was released through the "*Night Film* Decoder" app.[5] As it was originally conceived, the app allowed the reader to take a photo of a specific bird symbol that is next to some of the multimodal elements of the novel. Through that photo she would gain access to a supplementary file that for one reason or another could not be included in the novel itself.[6] In other words, through this app, the reader would be able to interact with some multimodal elements of the text in their original and intended forms. These elements of the novel are no longer restricted to paper and ink but rather remain code with which the reader can interact. We can watch a trailer for one of Cordova's films, *Lovechild*, and we can hear a doctor from the psychiatric institute Ashley was a patient of recount the brief disappearance of Cordova's

---

5. This app is no longer functional, but, as we shall see, the information contained in it can still be found on Pessl's (2014b) website.

6. I was not able to use a version of the app, but instead have read various accounts of it: Marie-Laure Ryan's (2016: 346) "Digital Narrative: Negotiating a Path between Experimental Writing and Popular Culture"; NPR's (2013) "App, Secret Sites Create the Immersive World of 'Night Film'"; and Maggie Lange's (2013) "Leave Easter Eggs out of My Books, Please."

daughter from the hospital. We, the readers, then, are no longer constrained by the material pages of the novel and can experience these aspects of the world produced by *Night Film* firsthand. The app and the transmedial augmentations it contained allowed the reader to get as close to a Ryan-esque level of literal immersion as possible, a level that the pages of the novel are unable to produce. As Ryan (2016: 347) herself notes with regard to the app: "For those readers who become immersed in the novel, the augmentations are a way of pushing back the moment when they will be expelled from the storyworld."

And yet, the app itself appears to have been short-lived. In the first edition of the novel (2013) there was a note at the end of the text before the acknowledgments page that informed readers of the app. In the reading group edition printed a year later (2014), however, this note has been removed, suggesting that the app was already gone—or close to it—by that time. While the app itself and its scanning feature are no longer available, all of the supplemental augmentations are listed on Pessl's website along with the corresponding page number and name of the multimodal aspect they accompany. And so, while these supplementations are still accessible, they no longer require physical interaction with the text itself to access them. The removal of the app, though, begs the question of why such an addition would be so unsuccessful, especially since the novel itself contains many multimodal aspects and, as we have seen, is preoccupied with the question of immersion, a question ostensibly answered by the app. Pessl herself may have inadvertently given us a clue as to the cause of the ultimate downfall of the app in an interview with NPR (2013): "Ideally you will read the book, and if you want to continue the experience, that's when you find out about the app, and you can get additional content in that way. But it is certainly not something that you need to do while you're reading, because I love the immersive reading experience, and I did not want to interrupt that in any way with technology." The app, then, was designed not as a part of the reading experience but as an afterword to it. Indeed, to engage with it while reading would be an "interruption" to the novel's immersion. And so, while the other multimodal elements that are enclosed within the novel further the plot or expand Cordova's world, the artifacts contained in the app merely allow the reader to pretend for a few more minutes that Cordova and his films are real. The closest we get to one of these films, though, is the short trailer for *Lovechild* and some retro-styled posters for the other films. The films themselves remain out of reach.

Beyond the content of the supplemental materials, it is their extratextual, transmedial form that poses the biggest problem. By existing outside of the text itself, these artifacts attempt to actualize the world of the novel and, by extension, the reader's immersion in it. As we've discussed, this app—or even just the list on the website—is a form of Ryan's "corporeal experience" where the reader can actively engage with the world of the text. This engagement, though, undermines the novel's formal interrogation of immersion. For, while in terms of the thematic content the reader is invited in, in terms of form and structure that invitation is rescinded. By tearing up the invitation, the form of the novel marks a certain indifference to the presence of the reader—we can watch the party through the window but cannot go inside. It is this conflict between content and structure that allows the novel to interrogate immersion and, more precisely, the reader's role in defining the immersiveness of a text. The novel highlights a conflict between readerly experience and textual form; the app, on the other hand, succumbs completely to the whims of the reader, who can meander through the novel jumping from bird icon to bird icon, listening, watching, reading, or even skipping the extra content. Post-app, she doesn't even need the book at all and instead can click through the list on the website, completely removed from the text itself.

What this conflict between app and text highlights, then, is that there are two distinct forms of immersion at work within the novel. These forms go beyond the questions of literal or representational, thematic or structural, and instead are dependent upon how the actual experience of the reader is defined. To rephrase, is the central immersive experience of a reader that of the world of the text or that of the mechanical process of reading itself? The three theories of immersion we have discussed, and indeed even the beginning of our discussion itself, assumes that the readerly experience of a novel is the engagement of a reader with the world of the text. The level and type of engagement with that world is certainly different for Ryan than it is for Ercolino, but the underlying centrality of that world is the same. That being said, Ercolino's object of study—long, intricate novels—does require a consideration of the act of reading itself and, more specifically, how a novel is able to compel a reader to keep turning hundreds or even over a thousand pages.

Part of that compulsion, according to Ercolino, is the reader's desire to be able to finally connect the dots laid out by the novel's paranoid imagination as well as its quest to be a totality of the real. A subsequent part of this readerly compulsion, though, is the maximization of the materiality of the text itself. Indeed, novels of substantial length have had their page count become a sizable aspect of their marketing campaigns.[7] As Ercolino (2015: 23) underscores:

> The maximalist novel would seem to be . . . one of the most refined literary products of late capitalism. Hundreds and hundreds of pages and some hefty weight, its status as a commodity is unequivocally confirmed at a sensorial level. . . . [It is] a commodity item that takes up a good bit of shelf space in bookstores, which is impressive because of its physical size, and certainly not because it is a highly sophisticated literary product.

In other words, the literal weight of a maximalist novel is a central aspect of its appeal as a commodity, its appeal to not a reader but a consumer. Ercolino reads this appeal as a fetishistic response to the late capitalist mantra of quantity over quality. And while this fetishism is no doubt true, the length of a novel is not only mere decoration meant to catch a buyer's eye. Once a buyer becomes a reader, the material weight of the book is no longer just a selling point but an integral part of the experience of reading it.

It is this tangible experience of reading that Pessl did not want interrupted by the app. The "immersive reading experience" she is guarding cannot be that of the world of the novel, for if it was then the app would not disrupt but deepen the experience. This experience is instead that of the book itself, an experience that can only be obtained via the process of reading. In essence, then, the ink and paper that alienate us from the world of the novel and thereby appear to hinder our immersion (into Cordova's world), are in actuality necessary for our immersion (into reading). To put a finer point on it, *Night Film*'s continuous reminders of its own materiality that are built into its form and structure are not a refusal of immersion but rather an invitation for a different type of immersion. And this type of immersion, unlike that of the reader into the world of the text, does not depend upon any subjective responses of the reader, for immersion into the reading of the text depends only upon the novel itself. In other words, this type of immersion is structurally similar to Carroll's conception of art-horror, in that it is a normative experience dictated by the structure of the novel and is indifferent to any actual experience of individual readers.[8]

---

7. Ercolino highlights the advertisements for *Infinite Jest*, but we could also think of the discussion around the increasing page count of the *Harry Potter* series, as well as any of Stephen King's recent novels.

8. The experience of reading here is not how a specific person reads a text—in an armchair by the window for example—but rather the experience that is dictated by the structure of the novel itself. This experience is dependent upon the interplay between a novel's structure, content, and materiality. In the case of *Night Film*, this experience is largely produced via the conflict between the novel's multimodal structure and intense awareness of its own materiality as a book, in that the reader is consistently reminded of and recentered in the text itself.

Moreover, this type of immersion is accessible only through books, as opposed to any medium that tells a story or builds a world. This medium specificity is especially important when considered in terms of the horror genre, as many of the generic conventions that mark contemporary horror films do not translate well onto the page. The two most prominent examples are gore and jump-scares, both of which are designed to elicit a visceral response in the viewer, a response that counterintuitively highlights a viewer's level of engagement by how far she recoils from the screen. Jump-scares are incompatible with the textual form, as the necessary surprise and magnitude of sight or sound required to cause a viewer to physically react cannot be achieved with ink and paper.[9] Gore, on the other hand, can be described in a novel, though that description will usually be in the form of words—and perhaps an image or two if the novel is multimodal. Reading about gruesome killings or maimings, however, is not the same as "seeing" them on screen.

Take, for example, an incident given to us thirdhand in *Night Film,* during which Cordova exploits his own son's tragic dismemberment near the set for one of his films:

> The boy was holding the bloody fingers in his hand, screaming in pain, asking his father if he could call an ambulance.
> The director said no. Instead, he fired one of the actors and made his son play the part.
> The director had his son shoot sixteen complete takes before the boy went unconscious. An ambulance was finally called, but by then too much time had elapsed to reattach the fingers.
> . . . The devastating pain on Theo's face is real and if you stop the film exactly at the 5:48″ mark you can see the raw bone of the severed fingers on his left hand dangling there. (Pessl 2014a: 184–85)

We read of this incident with McGarth via a reproduction of a restricted Cordova fan site, the "Blackboards," which includes a blurry black-and-white still from the film in question that clearly shows a young man missing part of his left index finger, middle finger, and thumb (fig. 2). While this story includes all the relevant and gory details: screams of pain, bloody severed fingers, and dangling raw bone, the visceral impact of these details is minimal. The frequent paragraph breaks, the repetitive sentence structure, and the placement of the still at the beginning

---

9. The closest a text could come to a jump-scare would be through a multimodal pop-up book that includes pictures and pop-ups that are designed to startle the reader. For example, there are pop-up versions of Edgar Allen Poe's "The Raven," AMC's *The Walking Dead*, and Bram Stoker's *Dracula*.

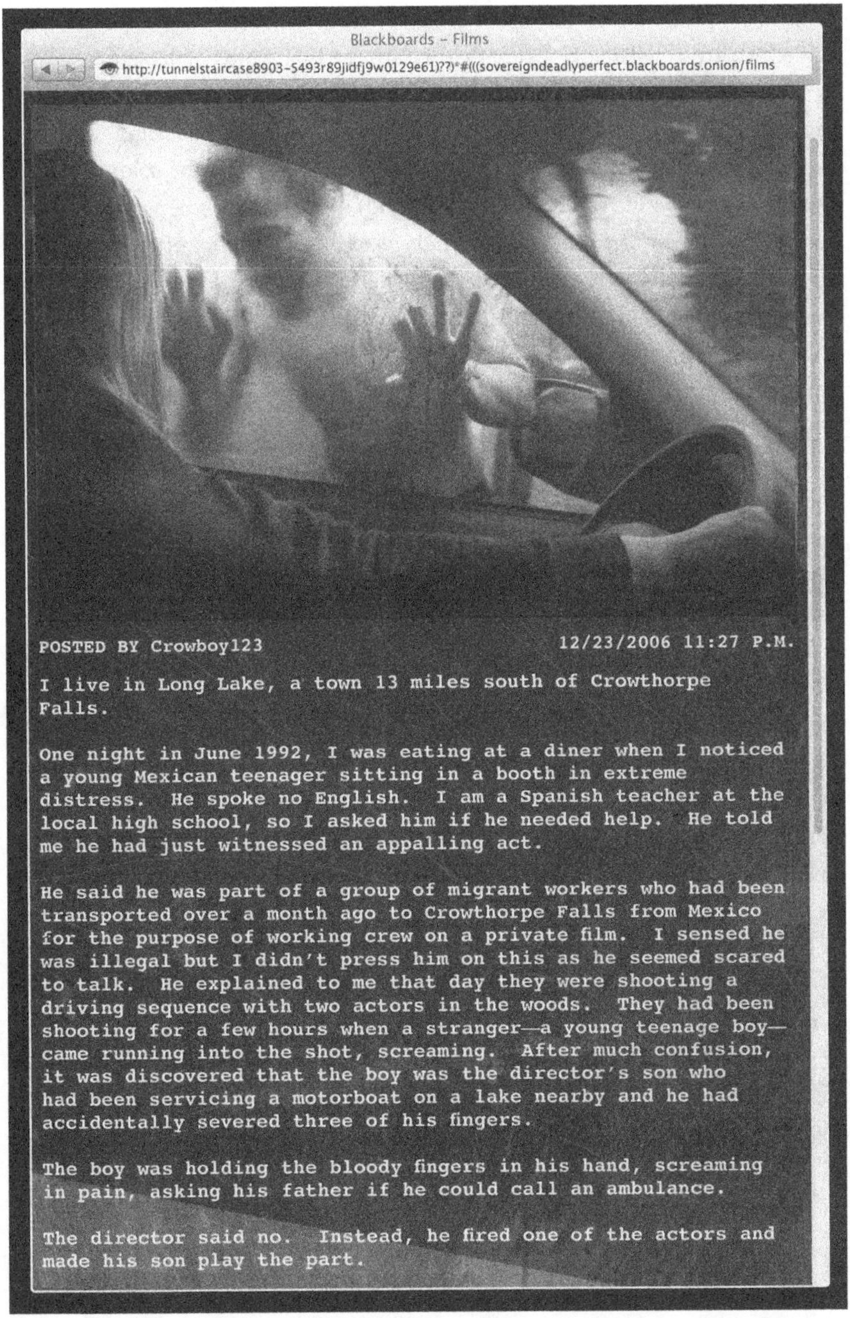

Blackboards - Films

http://tunnelstaircase8903-5493r89jidfj9w0129e61)??)*#(((sovereigndeadlyperfect.blackboards.onion/films

POSTED BY Crowboy123 12/23/2006 11:27 P.M.

I live in Long Lake, a town 13 miles south of Crowthorpe Falls.

One night in June 1992, I was eating at a diner when I noticed a young Mexican teenager sitting in a booth in extreme distress. He spoke no English. I am a Spanish teacher at the local high school, so I asked him if he needed help. He told me he had just witnessed an appalling act.

He said he was part of a group of migrant workers who had been transported over a month ago to Crowthorpe Falls from Mexico for the purpose of working crew on a private film. I sensed he was illegal but I didn't press him on this as he seemed scared to talk. He explained to me that day they were shooting a driving sequence with two actors in the woods. They had been shooting for a few hours when a stranger—a young teenage boy—came running into the shot, screaming. After much confusion, it was discovered that the boy was the director's son who had been servicing a motorboat on a lake nearby and he had accidentally severed three of his fingers.

The boy was holding the bloody fingers in his hand, screaming in pain, asking his father if he could call an ambulance.

The director said no. Instead, he fired one of the actors and made his son play the part.

Figure 2. Web page in Marisha Pessl's *Night Film* (2014a: 184). This image is a scan of the book itself.

of the account, all lessen the effect of these words and the brutality they depict. Rather, we are consistently aware that we are reading words on a page.

Indeed, this story is the conclusion of an eighteen-page spread of reproduced web pages from the Blackboards. Much like the web pages at the beginning of the novel, these are also realistic representations; albeit this time the color scheme is inverted (white words on a black background) to mark that it is part of the dark web. This visually jarring section reminds us of the materiality of the book in our hands and by so doing regrounds us in the reading process. Unlike a comparable scene in a horror film, then, this textualized scene of blood and bone does not beckon us into itself but rather highlights its own textuality to immerse us in the experience of reading.

This form of immersion does not depend upon any of the reader's subjective responses to the text but instead is an integral part of the act of reading. Therefore, the structural elements of the novel that solicit this type of immersion are the defining factors that determine whether or not the novel is successfully immersive. For the horror genre, then, this medium-specific immersion shifts the focus from the content of the novel (what would make us jump in fear or recoil in disgust) to its form and structure (how the text is presented to us and how this presentation compels us to continue reading). By so doing, this immersive focus on the experience of reading highlighted by the novel seeks to imagine and represent a distinction between the experience of reading a book and the experience of watching a film. *Night Film*, then, despite its title and the centrality of Cordova's work, is only interested in the medium of film as it serves as a foil to that of the novel. In fact, in every instance where the materiality of the book reasserts itself, the autonomy of the structure of the experience of reading is further underscored by the irony of the novel's title.

Moreover, this distinction between film and novel,[10] as well as the form of immersion put forth by it, rejects the scare factory version of the horror genre. *Night Film* aligns this scare factory and its reliance on emotional responses with the medium of film through the various reactions to Cordova's oeuvre depicted by it. Through this alignment, Pessl's novel criticizes horror films for their reliance on the reactions of a primarily male audience. Hence, it is no coincidence that

---

10. My argument is not about this difference, nor does it take a stand for or against either medium. Rather, I am interested in Pessl's representation of this difference for the purposes of her novel.

the narrator, Scott McGarth, is a man. After all, from the pinnacle work of Carol Clover (1996) that interrogates how and why a male-dominated audience is able to identify with a slasher film's "final girl" to recent statistics about moviegoers,[11] the horror film has been understood as male dominated and male centered both in terms of production and reception. And while the gender gap is lessening on both fronts, the "male gaze" remains a primary facet of the genre and its filmic conventions—one only has to compare the fate and wardrobe of female victims to that of their male counterparts to see this feature at work. This male gaze is produced twofold in Pessl's novel: first, in the horror director Stanislas Cordova, and secondly in the narrator, Scott McGarth. It is this second literal and representational male gaze that largely serves as a foil to the novel's larger structure. Though it may initially seem as though we are meant to identify with McGarth as we read web pages and other multimodal artifacts over his shoulder, that identification is quickly negated by the materiality of the text itself. Through McGarth, then, Pessl not only equates the scare factory version of horror with film but also genders it male.

But of course, *Night Film,* despite its title, is not a film but a novel. And where the audience for not only horror films but most mainstream films in general is characteristically male driven, the audience for novels is characteristically female, as 80 percent of American readers are women.[12] *Night Film*'s equating of books with a normative immersive experience, therefore, engenders this experience as female. And so, while Pessl's work is largely uninterested in feminized or gendered thematics as such, through her staging of the question of immersion, artistic autonomy itself becomes a feminist claim. For McGarth's male gaze as he stares at the obituary picture of Cordova's daughter as if she is a victim that he can retroactively save is interrupted by the paper and ink we are holding. This structural disruption of the masculinization stereotypically associated with the horror movie is what underscores the feminism of *Night Film*'s ambition to autonomy.

This feminism of Pessl's novel, then, while tangential to Clover's claims about gender in horror and in particular in slasher films, is an attempt not to regender the genre but rather to use the accepted gender politics of horror (and

11. For a more detailed breakdown of recent horror movie audiences, see Rubin 2018.

12. See editorials in the *Guardian* and NPR entitled "Without Women the Novel Would Die" (2019) and "Why Women Read More Than Men" (2007), respectively, as well as Helen Taylor's recent book, *Why Women Read Fiction: The Stories of Our Lives* (2019).

especially horror films) to highlight the novel's claim to artistic autonomy. *Night Film* uses the male gaze central to Clover and others as the exemplary form of solicited audience engagement that it subsequently disavows. Clover, on the other hand, is interested not in disavowing this male gaze but rather in pinpointing it as the driving force behind the ostensible feminism of a trope like the final girl, who is not only the sole survivor when the credits roll but also fights back against or even kills the male villain. Clover argues that the final girl's journey from victim to hero is also a process of regendering this character from female to male—or at least less female. And so, this supposed symbol of girl power is not quite as feminist as she first appears. In Clover's account the structural and thematic context of this character (from camera angles to unmistakably phallic weapons) is what prohibits her from becoming a true feminine heroine, as opposed to a stand-in for a male hero.

Pessl is not interested in any sort of redemptive feminism of horror and its tropes but instead positions the novel form as a foil to the masculinization that is seemingly inherent to the filmic medium. She does not wish to present a "female gaze" that would simply flip the gender of the intended audience—or at least the gender to which that audience is meant to identify—but rather seeks to disrupt this type of identification all together. For Pessl, this disruption is achieved through the replacement of film and its gendered gaze with paper and ink. And so, while the novel is told through a male point of view, the way it is formally structured obstructs any possible identification with that point of view by the reader. McGarth's role as a stand-in for the ideal horror audience is both acknowledged by the content of his narration and disrupted by its form.

It is via a focus on the experience of reading itself and the novelistic structure necessary to maintain that focus that *Night Film* resists the lure of repetitive and cliché scares, while still being a horror novel. Pessl's redefining of immersion unbinds horror from any emotional responses it elicits. This does not mean, of course, that those emotional responses—or even the desire for them—goes away; for if they did, what would distinguish horror from any other genre? Rather, these subjective responses are no longer the determining factor of a horror text's immersiveness but are instead one possible response to that immersion. For, immersion itself is independent of any subjective reactions from readers and instead relays on a normative understanding of the text's structure.

Melissa C. Macero is a PhD candidate in English literature at the University of Illinois at Chicago, specializing in twentieth- and twenty-first-century American literature and film with a concentration in popular culture, horror studies, and critical theory. Her dissertation explores the aesthetics of the horror genre and in particular the genre's imagined relationship to an audience, from Henry James to contemporary slashers.

Works Cited

Adorno, Theodor W. (1970) 1997. *Aesthetic Theory.* Translated by Robert Hullot-Kentor. Minneapolis: University of Minnesota Press.

Bean, Travis. 2020. "What Is the Scariest Movie Ever? Science Now Has an Answer to That Question." *Forbes*, October 17. www.forbes.com/sites/travisbean/2020/10/17/what-is-the-scariest-movie-ever-well-science-now-has-an-answer-to-that-question/.

Carroll, Noël. 1990. *Philosophy of Horror; or, Paradoxes of the Heart.* New York: Routledge.

Church, David. 2021. *Post-horror: Art, Genre, and Cultural Elevation.* Edinburgh: Edinburgh University Press.

Clover, Carol J. 1996. *Men, Women, and Chainsaws: Gender in the Modern Horror Film.* London: British Film Institute.

Ercolino, Stefano. 2015. *The Maximalist Novel: From Thomas Pynchon's "Gravity's Rainbow" to Roberto Bolaño's "2666."* Translated by Albert Sbragia. New York: Bloomsbury.

Hawkins, Joan. 2000. *Cutting Edge: Art-Horror and the Horrific Avant-garde.* Minneapolis: University of Minnesota Press.

Lange, Maggie. 2013. "Leave Easter Eggs out of My Books, Please." *Gawker*, August 22. www.gawker.com/leave-easter-eggs-out-of-my-books-please-1184113859.

NPR. 2013. "App, Secret Sites Create the Immersive World of *Night Film*." August 19. www.npr.org/sections/alltechconsidered/2013/08/19/213518390/app-secret-sites-create-the-immersive-world-of-night-film.

Pessl, Marisha. 2014a. *Night Film.* New York: Random House.

Pessl, Marisha. 2014b. "*Night Film* Decoder." www.marishapessl.com/night-film-app/.

Rubin, Rebecca. 2018. "Diverse Audiences Are Driving the Horror Box Office Boom." *Variety*, October 26. www.variety.com/2018/film/box-office/horror-movies-study-1202994407/.

Ryan, Marie-Laure. 2015. *Narrative as Virtual Reality 2: Revisiting Immersion and Interactivity in Literature and Electronic Media.* Baltimore: Johns Hopkins University Press.

Ryan, Marie-Laure. 2016. "Digital Narrative: Negotiating a Path between Experimental Writing and Popular Culture." *Comparative Critical Studies* 13, no. 3: 331–52.

Taylor, Helen. 2019. *Why Women Read Fiction: The Stories of Our Lives.* Oxford: Oxford University Press.

Thomas-Corr, Johanna. 2019. "Without Women the Novel Would Die: Discuss." *Guardian*, December 7. www.theguardian.com/books/2019/dec/07/why-women-love -literature-read-fiction-helen-taylor.

Weiner, Eric. 2007. "Why Women Read More Than Men." NPR, September 5. www.npr .org/templates/story/story.php?storyId=14175229.

The Mom and the Many:
Animal Subplots and Vulnerable Characters
in *Ducks, Newburyport*

BEN DE BRUYN

1. Introduction: Sitting Ducks

Cementing her reputation as a writer of innovative fiction, Lucy Ellmann's *Ducks, Newburyport* (2019) is an ambitious encyclopedic novel that updates modernist strategies for the twenty-first century while showing that human plots and nonhuman subplots can no longer be disentangled at a time when animals are exposed to pollution, function as overworked laborers, and eke out an existence at the edge of extinction. The main character's meandering thoughts about a family cat illustrate the novel's themes and formal strategies:

> the fact that Frederick's luxuriating over there . . . , the fact that nobody can resist bending to talk to him and pat him, . . . but he doesn't *need* their pats, . . . he's not even noticing birds rustling nearby, . . . the fact that he's not thinking about the end of the world, . . . no sirree, . . . he's just thinking about his own life and he thinks it's swell, . . . the fact that I think animals think a lot, . . . they're the ones who have the *time*, . . . the fact that birds could think up whole novels in twenty seconds, I bet, livelier novels than Anne Tyler's too, . . . the fact that it's unbelievable but every single thing alive has its own . . . point of view, even a worm, or a jellyfish, . . . even a leaf has feelings, . . . the fact that all I want to do is achieve a little *contentment* . . . (Ellmann 2019a: 794–96)

This passage helps to position *Ducks, Newburyport* in the literary field via the reference to Anne Tyler, celebrated writer of novels like *Breathing Lessons* (1988) and *Redhead by the Side of the Road* (2020). Ellmann's protagonist appreciates her brand of domestic realism; she would like to read "an Anne Tyler" (Ellmann 2019a: 788) because these novels about American middle-class life feature "close families" and are "sort of calming, because you know nothing too awful's going

Genre, Vol. 54, No. 2   July 2021
DOI 10.1215/00166928-9263104   © 2021 by University of Oklahoma

to happen" (790). Echoing existing critiques that categorize her as a conservative writer, however, the main character adds that "Anne Tyler's from Baltimore,
world HQ of the KKK, . . . but her books aren't about that" and that her characters
"scrape a living rinsing bottles or something unambitious like that, that you can't
believe a person can make a living out of, kind of like baking *pies*" (790). These
remarks establish parallels with *Ducks, Newburyport*, which likewise centers on
domestic life and a downwardly mobile protagonist who is a semiprofessional pie
maker. But the allusions to racism, capitalism, and the end of the world intimate
that Ellmann's novel fits into a divergent literary project, which does not shy away
from structural violence. The protagonist's speculations about animal minds and
fast "bird novels" further suggest that her narrative differentiates itself by aban-
doning the "slow pace" of Tyler's books (791) and making room for nonhuman
perspectives, the central topic of this article.

Though its manifold digressions make the text hard to summarize, *Ducks,
Newburyport* tells the story of two mothers living in Ohio in the early months of
2017: an unnamed housewife who worries about her four children while baking
countless pies and a wild mountain lion who makes dangerous forays into human
territory in search of her missing cubs. The basic message is accordingly straightforward: "Moms are *important*, even if nobody else thinks so" (94). The human
plot narrates routine occurrences like family meals, trips to the store, and the
attempt to deliver numerous batches of pies but also dramatic episodes involving
a flash flood, a runaway child, and an attempted home-jacking. These events are
hard to identify and follow, however, as they are backgrounded by the housewife's
monologue, which records her train of thought in a single sentence that spans
almost one thousand pages, has no chapter or even paragraph breaks, and is composed of innumerable subclauses introduced by the phrase "the fact that." This
stream of consciousness voices practical concerns about housework and crippling
medical debt alongside lingering grief over the untimely death of the protagonist's parents. But it also mimics digital platforms in zigzagging between random
subjects like musicals, nuclear codes, and decluttering gurus as well as urgent
topics like #MeToo, #BlackLivesMatter, and the polarizing Trump presidency.
Though this remarkable monologue points in disparate directions, its centrifugal
digressions are reined in by centripetal themes and leitmotifs, in line with Stefano
Ercolino's (2014) account of the dual tendencies at work in maximalist literature.
In terms of theme, the novel accentuates past and present forms of violence in
the United States, with an emphasis on aggression toward women and ecologi-

cal endangerment, as illustrated by the mountain lion plot. In doing so, it brings to mind the fact that "slow violence" is an apt descriptor of "domestic abuse" in addition to systemic pollution, according to Rob Nixon (2011: 3, 16). The spiral is an example of the text's leitmotifs, for this shape is linked to phenomena ranging from flowers and computers (Ellmann 2019a: 709) over the mother's negative thought process (677, 729, 911) to the course of the lion's journey (630, 801, 945) and other animal minds: "Do gorillas talk to themselves all the time like we do, . . . I don't know . . . but *I* think in . . . dizzying spirals" (288). Through such refrains, the text clarifies its own form and unifies its materials; the mother makes "spiraling pastries while I myself spiral out of control like a whirling dervish" (495) and keeps "spiraling into a panic about my mom and animal extinctions and the Second Amendment" (515).

Ducks, Newburyport participates in two literary traditions that are relevant to my argument about its nonhuman imagination. Though its experimental energy chafes against the narrow parameters of identifiable subgenres, Ellmann's novel is a form of climate fiction, for it addresses the "sixth mass extinction" (317), a flash flood triggered by "climate change" (593), and the subculture of "preppers" (186, 604). The narrative does not conjure up apocalyptic futures, however, nor does it overlook the uneven culpabilities and vulnerabilities of distinct human communities. It rather evokes what Stephanie LeMenager (2017: 225–26) calls the "everyday Anthropocene," in which characters pursue "a project of staying home and, in a sense distant from settler-colonialist mentalities, *making* home of a broken world." Because of its encyclopedic approach, it is also a textbook example of Heather Houser's (2020) "infowhelm" texts, creative works that integrate and interrogate ecological data. If the content of Ellmann's novel points toward climate literature, its form reconnects with modernism. For its epic stream of consciousness recalls both Woolf's *Mrs Dalloway* (1925) and Joyce's *Ulysses* (1922), and Ellmann (2019b) herself has stated that, while "it's nice of people to take an interest in new writing," "everybody knows readers would get more from reading *Ulysses* or Woolf." In addition, she is the daughter of two critics who published groundbreaking accounts of feminist literature and James Joyce—and there are conspicuous similarities between these figures and the narrator's parents in *Ducks, Newburyport*. The novel is consequently an exemplar of "metamodernism," the trend in which the "experiments . . . of twentieth-century modernist culture have acquired new relevance to the moving horizon of contemporary literature" (James and Seshagiri 2014: 88). It follows from these observations that Ellmann's text is akin to works such as Eimear McBride's *A Girl Is a Half-Formed Thing* (2013) and Mike McCormack's *Solar Bones* (2016), as well as Barbara Kingsolver's *Unsheltered* (2018) and Jenny Offill's *Weather* (2020). Yet it also performs a remarkable experiment with animal subplots, as this article will clarify.

The position of *Ducks, Newburyport* can be triangulated by investigating its remarks about another writer and summarizing its form and themes. But we may also opt for a route that is closer in spirit to this encyclopedic book and trace one of its leitmotifs, "sitting ducks." Ducks are mentioned several times; they make an involuntary appearance in the housewife's favorite restaurant, for instance, and are involved in a dangerous incident from her mother's past set in Newburyport. Readers also repeatedly encounter the phrase "sitting ducks," a famous idiomatic expression that refers to something or someone who is vulnerable to attack. The housewife uses the phrase to capture the emotional complexity of family life, in remarks on her first husband and his current absence from the life of his daughter Stacy, who is "stuck in limbo, sitting duck, waiting for Frank's next move" (Ellmann 2019a: 347). The expression returns in reflections on the mother's past professional life as a history professor and her current, equally thankless job as a pie maker. The first job was bad because "it wasn't minimum wage but pretty close, . . . the fact that you're a sitting duck if you're part-time" (811), and the second exposes her to criticism about her baking efforts and "unless you're upbeat enough, . . . you're just a sitting duck" (400). The leitmotif crops up again in a brutal scene of domestic violence involving her best friend: "[Cathy] was really a sitting duck in that car, the fact that he could've killed her easy" (757). And it reappears in descriptions of real-life events that happened in Zanesville and Gnadenhutten and involved the execution of escaped zoo animals—"[The owner] kept them all in tiny cages . . . and [the animals] were all in just terrible shape, sitting ducks for those police marksmen" (838)—and the slaughter of no fewer than ninety-six unarmed Native American people in 1782—"The Moravian Indians were just 'sitting ducks,' . . . they were all pacifists so they didn't put up a fight" (329). As this overview demonstrates, ducks are mentioned in the context of food and labor, past and present family issues, and unrelenting violence toward women, Indigenous people, and animals—the signature concerns of this novel.

But I will single out another passage because it again points toward the novel's sustained exploration of nonhuman life. As the next sections explicate more fully, *Ducks, Newburyport* pushes us to contemplate the lives and worlds of other creatures. Though this passage centers on plants instead of animals, it provides another illustration of how the narrative integrates anecdotes about other forms of fragile life and their alien points of view:

> that tree out back . . . that came down . . . last fall . . . now has branches starting to grow out of its side, . . . the fact that David Attenborough's always talking about tree competition in the rainforest, as if trees are . . . thrilled when any nearby tree dies, . . . Our Approach to School Bullying, but maybe there's also . . . tree empathy, . . . they're often siblings as well, . . . the fact that if a nearby tree's injured . . . , the other trees *feed* it . . . if that's true it means trees sort of think, and plan, and care, . . . "mommy trees," . . . the fact that maybe our trees have been missing their pal over there . . . , and they've been quietly *feeding* it some-how, underground, . . . maybe there's more going on in [trees] tha[n] we thought, . . . the fact that trees go into a dormant state at night, . . . if trees sleep, perchance they dream, . . . maybe they have wish-fulfilment dreams about abundant water sources, . . . they're just sitting ducks, . . . they can't get away . . . (714–16)

Repeating the "sitting ducks" refrain, this characteristic digression is prompted by the fallen tree and ponders its resurgent vitality in a way that underscores the precarious nature of plant life and its difference from human modes of embodi-ment ("they can't get away"). But it also discards reductive accounts of nonhu-man competition for more imaginative views of plants and plant networks that draw on biology ("dormant state") and literature (Shakespeare's "perchance to dream") to speculate about tree perception and hypothesize about the parallels between human mothers, bullies, and siblings and their vegetal counterparts. And these analogies already hover in the background, seeing that the mother describes humans as sitting ducks throughout the novel. While the sweeping narrative of *Ducks, Newburyport* can be approached from various critical angles, this article will focus on its systematic inclusion of similar episodes about nonhuman worlds. This strategy is on display in the cougar narrative, but a closer analysis unveils a wide array of animal characters, all of which highlight human violence and promote a more convivial, "neighborly" mode of cohabitation with other critters.

2. Animals, Narratives, Characters

Before scrutinizing the menagerie of *Ducks, Newburyport*, we should contextual-ize its approach to multispecies storytelling by reviewing pertinent insights about extinction, narrative, and gender as well as anecdotes, characters, and attention. First, the human mother's monologue regularly addresses the vanishing of non-human species, and this means that Ellmann's novel participates in extinction discourse. As Ursula Heise asserts in *Imagining Extinction* (2016), the current, alarming decline of biodiversity prompts both cultural and biological questions. The efforts of conservation science will only have an impact, she writes, when "the species with whom we co-inhabit the planet . . . become part of the stories that human communities tell about themselves" (Heise 2016: 5), stories about their "history, modernization, and futures, as well as about their relation to [particular] species" (237). If we want to foster "multispecies justice" (6), we accordingly need to ask ourselves difficult questions about the limits and affordances of particular storytelling formats. As Heise explains, most extinction narratives adopt a narrow lens and zoom in on the disappearance of a single charismatic species—often in the form of an endangered female specimen (38)—a loss that is taken to represent both the terminal state of the environment and the diminished state of the nation involved. According to Heise, this dominant strategy precludes hopeful alternatives and prioritizes wild creatures at the expense of less charismatic critters. Given that the planet is now "pervasively domesticated" (158), she further urges us to integrate occasionally clashing insights from environmental ethics and animal welfare so as to keep in view both wild and domesticated animals. These points resonate with *Ducks, Newburyport*, which foregrounds the fate of cougars and endangered creatures but contemplates domesticated animals and other forms of interspecies injustice, too.

If Heise's work clarifies the novel's preoccupation with extinction and violence, David Herman's primer in bionarratology illuminates its perspectival experiments. Three insights from *Narratology beyond the Human* (2018) are indispensable here. First, Herman elucidates how animal stories enable us to reimagine cultural ontologies, "Assumptions about what sorts of beings populate the world and how those beings' qualities and abilities relate to the qualities and abilities ascribed to humans" (2). As he describes, narratives can enlarge a restricted, anthropocentric view of the self and the person and redraw the boundaries of human families and spaces in a biocentric, more-than-human direction. Consequently, multispecies narratives confront us with animal selves, transhuman families, and overlapping, more-than-human geographies. Second, Herman builds on earlier publications in narratology and animal studies to develop new tools for the analysis of animal characters and focalizers, who are often rendered in ways that attempt to do justice to the *Umwelt* or unique sensory bubble inhabited by a particular animal species. Stories about nonhuman characters do not only unsettle narrow ontologies, in sum, but experiment with point of view to approximate the unfamiliar lifeworlds of other beings. Third, Herman maintains that narrative techniques introduced by modernist writers to evoke human minds were subsequently repurposed to capture conjectural animal worlds. In *Mrs Dalloway*, Woolf acts as an "intraspecies *Umwelt* explore[r], using methods of mind presentation to examine variations in the way . . . humans [experience] different phenomenal worlds" (Herman 2018: 153). But in her animal narrative *Flush* (1933), she "leverages modernist techniques as . . . a resource for modeling how the biophysical structure as well as the life histories of nonhuman agents might impinge on their [experiences of their] environments" (Herman 2018: 167). Herman's insights alert us to the more-than-human ontology, geography, and family of *Ducks, Newburyport*, and they further allow us to connect its animal theme more tightly to its quasi-modernist experiments with focalization (remember Frederick, the sleepy cat).

My argument is also in conversation with debates on gender and storytelling. Ellmann's novel directs attention to a human and an animal mother, and its two-pronged tale explicitly spotlights the interconnected oppressions of women and animals analyzed by ecofeminists. As Susan Fraiman (2012) has stressed, feminist scholars like Donna Haraway have developed alternative modes of animal storytelling, which privilege cross-species interactions (see Fraiman 2012). This tradition is rearticulated in a way that resonates with Ellmann's use of anecdotes in Vinciane Despret's *What Would Animals Say If We Asked the Right Questions?* In her "scientific fables," Despret ([2012] 2016: vii) jettisons reductive forms of animal science in favor of "anecdotes" told by "nonscientists [like] caregivers, trainers, breeders," seeing that these stories make animals more interesting and celebrate "the possibility of *surprising* the one who asks questions of them" (39). If we follow in the footsteps of animals and amateurs, theorems about male dominance, for instance, prove brittle; after monitoring a pack closely, a wolf specialist concludes that "there is no relation of dominance, only parents who guide the activities of their pups" (58). Inspired by such research, Despret pairs criticism with humor to promote "more curiosity, more attention, more hypotheses" (67). The ultimate goal is to "creat[e] other stories that offer a different future to 'companion species'" (190), stories that respect unfamiliar *Umwelten* but also acknowledge the "porosity" of worlds resulting from human-animal cohabitation (165). To Despret's mind, the belief that "animals can behave *otherwise*" (63) is supported by websites and YouTube clips, in which animals appear as "characters" (197) and beings "remarkable for their heroism, sociality, . . . intelligence, humor, unpredictability" (198). This argument again matches with

Ducks, Newburyport, for the novel reflects on gender and domesticity and incorporates surprising animal anecdotes that are often linked to the web: "I saw a YouTube video of a mongoose *screaming* at a pack of lions, . . . that was one brave mongoose" (Ellmann 2019a: 394–95). The mother's speculations about animals recall Despret's quirky aesthetic, moreover: "I wonder how a bee can stand its own buzz" (388); "I wonder if [dog language] varies a lot between . . . countries, or between breeds, like can Ethiopian dogs communicate easily with Argentinian dogs, or is it a slightly different dialect" (302).

The previous points about biodiversity, domesticity, and animal stories can be illustrated with the help of two characters from *Ducks, Newburyport*: Mr. President and the First Lady, two bald eagles who are monitored in real time by a nest camera in Washington, DC, like their real-life counterparts in the National Arboretum. Ellmann's protagonist follows this online feed: "We like the *eagle-cam*, . . . Gillian's keeping an eye on the eagle chicks with me this year" (245). In accordance with Heise's remarks, the story gestures toward the symbolical meanings of these creatures—"They live way up there in the treetops while the politicians tie themselves in knots down below" (245)—but it also mentions the "near-extinction" of the bald eagle at the hands of "hunters and farmers and egg-poachers" (924). Eagles are also forced to forage for food in a polluted world, as the housewife underlines, a former cancer patient herself: "People are still allowed to fish the Ohio but they're not supposed to *eat* what they catch, . . . the fact that *eagles* have to eat [river fish], whether they're safe or not, . . . an eagle can't just go out for chicken à la king" (323). The eaglecam also yields a longer anecdote:

> They had to rescue one of the DC eaglets because he got his leg caught between some twigs . . . they hoped at first he'd struggle free . . . but then they got scared he might starve, *on international live cam*, so some . . . park ranger guy . . . brought him down and they kept him under observation for a day or two but he was fine, . . . so they . . . put him back in the nest, the fact that the [guy] who carried him back up the tree, *kissed* the eaglet . . . before he left him there, which wasn't very professional but gosh, was it sweet, . . . the fact that I thought Mr. President and the First Lady might reject him, because of the smell of the park guy on him, but . . . everything's back to normal now, with raw pink fish for breakfast, lunch and dinner . . . (959–60)

This miniature narrative discloses the mother's concerns about family, food, and vulnerability. Indeed, she often associates these birds with domestic life; the eaglets remind her of aunt Abby (136), their parents bring to mind "Mommy and Daddy" (512), and "it always looks like one of [the eaglets] isn't getting any

[food], but it all seems to work out, . . . and all on raw fish torn to shreds for them by their devoted parents" (537). Such passages utilize the technique Herman (2018: 140) labels "Human-Source-Animal-Target" projections, in which "human motivations and practices [are] used as the basic template for interpreting non-human behavior" in order to "familiariz[e] . . . the target domain of animality" (153), in this case by representing unfamiliar eagle lives in terms of human experiences of food and family. Yet the anecdote also alludes to the independent lives of these animals, as it mentions their peculiar diet and surprising response to the eaglet's return. In addition, the anecdote speculates about their interior life, developing an earlier, self-reflexive comment: "There are seven and a half billion people . . . , so there must be seven and a half billion of these internal monologues going on, . . . the fact that animals must have some kind of monologue going on in *their* heads, . . . bald eagles certainly always seem to be thinking about something when you watch them on the eaglecam" (Ellmann 2019a: 514–15). In contrast to Anne Tyler's books, this text is a bird novel—or at least a *birdlike* novel. More generally, these eagles show that *Ducks, Newburyport* contemplates species extinction and animal worlds and deploys quirky anecdotes to establish cross-species ties between human and animal families living in a world scarred by fast as well as slow violence.

Two final points should be mentioned before returning to the novel. We have seen that Ellmann's text recounts unconventional anecdotes à la Despret: "There was a friendly squirrel once on our trash can . . . , at first . . . I thought I was befriending a wild animal, and maybe he'd become my pet squirrel . . . but then I got suspicious [and] got scared he got rabies, so I edged away and I never saw him again" (299). But some of these mininarratives are slowly fleshed out in the course of this long novel and task the reader with reconstructing particular animal "subplots"—a term that is usually employed to identify parallel storylines in plays but can be productively used and enriched in discussions of environmental themes. As David Letzler (2012: 313) observes, sprawling novels like *Infinite Jest* constitute valuable exercises in "mental filtering" because they "force us to navigate around their junk text to the text that is more important" (321). Similarly, Elizabeth Callaway (2018: 10) judges that *The Bone Clocks* is an important climate novel because "climate is presented as that which is right there in front of us if only we could filter out the noise of louder . . . stories" and this proves difficult in a text that deliberately misdirects attention toward other subjects. In other words, these long novels train readers to screen out junk text and heroic stories, so they are primed to track information that is crucial but easily overlooked. *Ducks, New-buryport* likewise uses animal subplots to exercise the reader's noticing skills, as the intermittent references to the eagles already indicated. Another important point is that Ellmann's novel is crowded with animal characters and makes good use of the tension between the individualized protagonist and the surrounding crowd of minor characters. As Alex Woloch has elaborated in *The One vs. the Many* (2003), novels distribute carefully calibrated portions of text to individual fictional characters, and this distribution of attention explains how underdeveloped secondary figures help prop up the protagonist's centrality. This basic distinction energizes the genre, Woloch (2003: 197) demonstrates, for minor figures perform vital roles, either by functioning as foils that clarify features or unfulfilled desires of the protagonist or by forming "competing centers of interest" that weaken our interest in the main character. The nineteenth-century novel is a crucial test case for the "character-system" (14), Woloch contends, because industrial capitalism promotes a hierarchical mindset, but the rise of democratic politics simultaneously fosters increasing attention to the lives of minor characters, *"the proletariat of the novel"* (27). This tension does not disappear in later fiction, however; our analysis of a novel like *Mrs Dalloway*, he asserts, "must begin with the remarkable way that the central protagonis[t] emerge[s] *out of* [a] previously minor positio[n]" (362). *Ducks, Newburyport* exploits the opportunities of the character-system, too, as the protagonist's centrality is put in relief by a long list of secondary figures including Julie Shriver, the Kinkels, and Ronny the stalker. But this article will foreground its minor *animal* characters instead because the inclusion of their subplots constitutes a significant intervention, I maintain, in an age when systemic human violence forces us to rethink how we include and exclude pets, wild creatures, and farm animals in our cultural narratives.

3. Jim, Adopted Dog

The next sections expand on my preliminary comments about *Ducks, Newbury-port* by tracking individual animals across its pages and reconstructing their violent worlds and independent subplots, organizing the material in a way that draws inspiration from publications by Joshua Bennett (2020) and Peter Brooks (2020). Like Bennett, I will examine the symbolical work of animal figures like dogs, cougars, and chickens in a context of violence and hope. As my analysis attends more closely to the subplots of individual animals, however, it splices his approach with Brooks's attempt to piece together the biographies of human characters invented by Balzac. More precisely, the following paragraphs profile Jim the dog, Mishipeshu the cougar, and, last but not least, the chickens Gracia and Audrey. Each of these animals operates as a foil for the human characters, especially the mother and her teenage daughter Stacy, but their stories also acquire a life of their own as the narrative proceeds and the text keeps circling back to the unenviable fate of animals—female animals especially—in today's world. As the analysis reveals, Ellmann's text entreats us to consider the distinct narrative roles, sensory worlds, and violent experiences of these characters, whose stories enrich the human plot and prompt grief alongside hope in an age of species extinction, animal cruelty, and industrial labor. While they are vulnerable "sitting ducks," too, these individuals act in surprising, hopeful ways as well.

Although the cougar is more prominent, Jim is the clearest example of a minor animal character in *Ducks, Newburyport*, as he leaves an indelible impression but remains peripheral to the main storyline. Jim's plot even allows the reader to inspect the device of the animal character, as it were, seeing that his exploits are narrated in one small part of the text; he only makes his first appearance at a late stage and rapidly disappears again from the main narrative. There is another reason why Jim is an exemplary minor character: he is a dog. As Ivan Kreilkamp has observed in *Minor Creatures* (2018), an account of nineteenth-century literature that builds on Woloch, animals usually star in brief anecdotes instead of more extended stories. The paradigmatic example is a dog:

> By midcentury, British newspapers and periodicals were filled with anecdotes . . . about . . . dogs; indeed, to be confined to . . . the anecdote would seem to define the Victorian dog's ambiguous position. Within the strictly delimited . . . form of the anecdote, even acts of bravery . . . cannot guarantee any lasting recognition; an animal "protagonist" of this particular genre possesses an individuality that [is] at once exceptional . . . and short-lived. . . . And so animal characters . . . operate . . . as reminders that those beings whom we individuate . . . can very easily slip back below the level of representability. (Kreilkamp 2018: 18–19)

Jim's subplot fits into this tradition, as it introduces a dog who is both unforgettable and quickly relegated to the sidelines. It also confirms Kreilkamp's broader point that pets perform a crucial symbolic function, seeing that sympathy for these prized animals humanizes readers and characters and sanctifies the home as a refuge from uncomfortably brutal forms of interspecies violence in the outside world. Because the children of Ellmann's protagonist have long wanted a pet dog (Ellmann 2019a: 63), she finally agrees to adopt Jim in the belief that "maybe we'd be more like a real family if we had a dog" (102). Her daughter also picked this dog for a reason, the mother suspects: "I personally think Stacy chose him for being the most unhappy dog at the pound" (851), and "it was kind of her to take pity on Jim" (867). He is a worthy object of human sympathy, we learn, in passages where the mother speculates about his inner world: "He's a . . . worried kind of dog, [and] cowers a lot, . . . I had to get the kids to stop trying to hug him . . . because it just makes him anxious" (848); "It's hard to imagine what he's thinking about, . . . maybe Jim is just shy, and I can sympathize, . . . the fact that looking at Jim, you begin to wonder if human beings are the only self-conscious animal" (850–51). As these remarks evince, the dog is treated as a family member, and even though he does not feel at home immediately, that paradoxically reinforces his centrality, as it connects him to the mother, who is unusually timid, too, and allows the mother and children of this transhuman family to train their cross-species sympathy. Not unlike the eagles, in sum, Jim contributes to the main plot by triggering extended reflections on domestic life and its emotional challenges.

Though he functions as a foil for the human characters, Jim also becomes a competing center of attention as a result of his semiautonomous subplot—and Ellmann's novel hence confirms the claims by Woloch and Kreilkamp that the attention to minor characters and minor creatures, respectively, gradually increases in literary history. As the narrative reveals, Jim encourages elaborate *Umwelt* speculation because he suffers from past trauma; the dog quickly disappears from the main storyline because he chooses to team up with the mountain lion; and he is adopted a second or even third time by the government tracker who finally manages to trap the cougar. The housewife is impressed by Jim's adventurous life and underlines its *narratable* quality, in an implicitly metafictional moment. Consider these excerpts, which reconstruct his subplot both before and after living with the narrator's family:

> Some twelve-year-old boys set fire to a dog shelter . . . on a dare, and fifty dogs suffocated, and our little Jim's one of the *survivors*, oh dear, . . . the horrors he's seen, . . . the fact that he never wags his tail . . . [he] was originally a farm pup, but he was no good at herding . . . so they dumped the poor guy at an animal shelter, which then *burnt down*, . . . the fact that he can hit a very high note . . . which is probably what saved him in the *fire*, because the firefighters heard him . . . (843, 848–49)

> [One of the children] saw the lion in our back yard . . . the same night Jim went missing, . . . what if . . . the lion . . . *ate* him . . . after we supposedly "rescued" him, . . . here's another news clip about the tracker, . . . and, oh . . . it's *Jim*, . . . the tracker says this is the dog that was hanging around with the lioness, . . . he looks so *happy* with the tracker guy, . . . if you think of all the things that one little dog's *been* through, a farm, a fire, a *lion*, . . . I just hope he didn't suffer, travel-

ing around with a lioness, . . . the fact that, sheesh, if your dog's so unhappy he'd
rather live with a *cougar*, it's . . . time to get a new dog . . . (922, 947–48)

These passages articulate that Jim stars in an exciting, independent subplot. It is
not entirely disconnected from the main narrative, for the housewife is likewise
traumatized by the past, and her rebellious daughter Stacy briefly goes missing, too—in fact, the mother accepts to adopt Jim to celebrate her safe return.
The Stacy connection again points toward structural violence against animals
(and women) because she decided to run away after her boyfriend "threatened
to kill her *cat*" when she refused his sexual advances (846). This interconnected
constellation of events underlines the double position of the pet as analyzed by
Kreilkamp: these animals are loved and adopted (and readopted) but also dumped
at shelters, burned alive, and threatened with execution. Even the mother's attitude is ambiguous. She worries about Jim from the start and feels bad about his
disappearance. Yet that does not stop her from thinking of a replacement: "Maybe
we can have one of Cathy's puppies, . . . Junie's about to give birth" (948). Her
response uncovers the limits of human sympathy and the precarious status of
pets, but the text also allows for a more positive reading. Because the dog seems
happier with the tracker, both the mother and her children feel that they should
abandon their claim to Jim's life, in line with observations that "dog owners . . .
never let their dogs do what they want" (849) and that police officers "dismis[s]
the yearnings of their dogs" (787). It might therefore be argued that this subplot
hints at a less possessive mode of pet ownership and human narrative control,
which accommodates the wayward desires and plots of creatures like Jim.

Through this character, the novel explores more-than-human domesticity,
unfamiliar mental worlds, and animal agency. But we should also notice that
Jim teams up with the cougar and crosses over to her subplot, which is narrated
in sections that are marked off from the housewife plot of *Ducks, Newburyport*.
As I explained, this dog is adopted by the human family and the tracker but also
by the lioness, who enters the housewife's garden at night, lured by the smell
of the chicken coop. She is thrown off guard by Jim's bark, which is "almost
like a lion's scream" (886), and abandons her designs on the chickens, but not
before making an unexpected friend. The scene is focalized through the cougar:
"[The dog] rolled on the ground to show he meant no harm [and] followed her
at a distance for days. . . . She became used to his abject shadow and [gradually]
stopped thinking about him" (886–87). The descriptions in these scenes confirm
the mother's reading of Jim's bashfulness: "the dog dreamt of fire and firemen"

(913) and "expect[ed] a beating" (927). But the crucial point is that Jim and the lioness become partners, perhaps even "friends" (977). She first considers attacking the dog and subsequently judges him to be "irrelevant" (887), yet he becomes "her dog companion" (913) and receives "a companionable swat" (926), despite the fact that cougars "never share" (407). After capturing the lioness, the tracker explains that "it was the dog's barking that gave them away" (943), yet in revealing their location, Jim probably saved the cougar from the armed posses that were pursuing her. These animals are intrigued by each other, furthermore; the cougar realizes "this dog was an oddity" (886) and the dog considers the lioness' behavior "more interesting . . . than all the rest of his life" (927). This multispecies curiosity is a defining trait of Jim more generally: "He's scared of people and other dogs, but he really seems to like the chickens" (848). While the dog's behavior is rooted in a history of violence, his subplot hence hints at a utopian form of multispecies collaboration—as articulated in Jim's recurrent adoption by the housewife, the cougar, and the tracker. What is more, his partnership with the lioness reterritorializes the storyworld's division between domestic and wild spaces as well as the textual boundary between the novel's human and animal plots. Through his semiferal story, this major minor character exposes the interspecies porosity of dog, human, and cougar worlds.

4. Mishipeshu, Fugitive Cougar

Ducks, Newburyport explores the social and narrative life of a pet dog, but it draws even more attention to a wild mountain lion. The novel recounts her experiences in vignettes that pepper the main narrative, and the resulting subplot mirrors the housewife storyline in various respects. Both mothers wake up at the outset, for instance, worry about food, witness the same flash flood, struggle to find missing children, and are threatened by armed men. Because of these structural parallels, the cougar ultimately functions as a "co-protagonis[t]" along the lines described by Woloch (2003: 245). This endangered creature is a symbolically resonant figure, moreover, and invites readings in terms of national identity and recent US politics. The lioness's journey produces "all kinds of . . . conspiracy theories . . . , #cougarcon, #pawgate, . . . Trump [is] tweeting that his enemies have released the lion to distract people from his important work, . . . now there's a *club*, devoted to shooting this one lion, [it] is called Freedom From Fear, the FFF, . . . after they get this lion, they're going to rid America of 'all predators, both human and animal'" (798–99). The lioness elicits other readings, too, seeing that the term "cougar" can refer to "older women who pursue . . . younger men" (Collard 2012a: 527), a usage that ultimately reinforces gender and species hierarchies by portraying female sexual freedom as predatory instinct. *Ducks, Newburyport* reclaims this cross-species link between women and mountain lions by downplaying sex and magnifying resilience. The result is not dissimilar to the process traced in Joshua Bennett's *Being Property Once Myself* (2020), in which African American writers "turn to the animal kingdom, that which had so often been used as a tool of their derision and punishment, as a site of futurity and fugitivity" (7). Obviously, we should not conflate distinct literary traditions and vastly different forms of injustice. Yet Bennett's account, which details how animal images do not only enable stereotyping and dehumanization but also make available a form of cross-species solidarity rooted in flight and tenacity, can be extrapolated to this context, especially seeing that he ponders less anthropocentric articulations of motherhood, too. Via the cougar subplot, *Ducks, Newburyport* again investigates unfamiliar vantage points and interspecies violence, as these sections are mostly focalized through the mountain lion and paint a picture of potential extinction and lifelong captivity for wild animals. These tragic notes are offset, however, by the subplot's hopeful arc, its multidirectional allegory, and its portrait of a nonviolent predator.

The cougar narrative seems tragic, for it elaborates the novel's shorter allusions to species extinction and the depleted environment of the contemporary United States. Granted, the lioness survives her journey, the cougar family is reunited in a zoo—"She had found her cubs and would lap them and love them and never let them go" (Ellmann 2019a: 959)—and the novel concludes with the housewife's plan to visit these animals. But Ellmann's text does not portray zoos as positive sites. One facility is the scene of a gruesome massacre, as I mentioned in the introduction, and the narrator remembers two dispiriting visits: "A lion tried to attack a baby through a glass window at a zoo in Utah . . . the lion looked awfully thin to me, and really serious about it" (112); "I once looked a mother orangutan right in the eye, when I took Stacy to some zoo . . . and we really seemed to connect for a moment, one mom to another, but then I left her there and never went back" (559–60). The lioness may rejoice when she recognizes her cubs, additionally, but the subsequent, immediate acceptance of a captive future jars with the first impression the zoo makes on this nonhuman focalizer: "The purpose of these [other] animals was no longer to exist for themselves—as was their right" (949). More importantly, Ellmann's novel does not return to these cougars after their reunion, and it ends shortly afterward, effectively implying that when these wild creatures become zoo animals their story is over. This elegiac conclusion is consistent with other passages that paint the lioness in a romanticized light. The housewife believes that it might even be a mistake to name this animal: "All her life that mountain lion has been alone and free and unnamed, and now she has a name and she's not free anymore" (944). The fact that the cougar vignettes are narrated in a distanced, third-person voice attests to a similar reluctance to incorporate this animal in human designs, though Kreilkamp (2018: 186) is surely right in noting that "any animal that is individuated . . . in a novel is thereby domesticated, brought into the realm of the human and so granted a status somewhat resembling that of a pet." Pets might become semiferal in this text, but cougars become semidomesticated, too.

In addition to its negative descriptions of zoos, *Ducks, Newburyport* pits humans and cougars against each other in the scenes focalized through the lioness. The third-person narrator who records her thoughts frames this focalizer as the natural ruler of a country now tragically overrun with humans. She is depicted as a "queen" (Ellmann 2019a: 93, 830) who rules "her land" (631, 830, 873) and is the true owner of the earth (93, 242, 407), in contrast to what humans believe: "[Men] thought it all belonged to them, but they were wrong" (631); "She would like to show [humans] who really ruled the world" (939); "The attention of [zoo visitors] did not much faze her: she was in her own world, an empire she made and carried with her" (949). These passages again use Human-Source-Animal-Target projections and apply human notions of property and aristocracy to the unfamiliar world of the cougar. They further reiterate the reductive template of most extinction stories, in which "the charismatic animal . . . comes to replace the human of high social standing who undergoes a tragic fall" (Heise 2016: 50–51). The cougar sections also employ the reverse strategy, "Animal-Source-Human-Target projections" (Herman 2018: 140), which defamiliarize our quotidian world via conjectural animal takes on human practices. In scenes focalized through the lioness, zoo animals appear as "lost hollow creatures" (Ellmann 2019a: 830) and "defeated" farm animals smell "of powerlessness and pain" (673). The cougar also contemplates "zooming balls of metal" (406), "cold metal cave[s]" (872), and "the noisy, smelly cars in which [humans] scarred their way across the earth" (913). Moreover, humans are incomprehensible creatures who possess "waggly mouths, from which poured a ceaseless variety of gurgles, cries and calls" (938) and ominously allow "males . . . to get . . . close to the young" (730). Humans even trespass on "lion territories that had long been demarcated" (496), as befits beings who desire "more dominance, more prey, and ever more territory" (830). In the final analysis, "They seemed wholly unaware of any being in the world besides themselves, and this . . . made them enemies of all" (730). These descriptions position humans against other animals, though they also allow readers of this text to take their blinkers off, paradoxically, and catch a glimpse of the cougar mind. And one reason for the text's elegiac effect is the suggestion that this richly rendered nonhuman perspective or "world" is threatened with extinction. As Vinciane Despret (2016: 166) observes in a related context, some animal worlds in our "pluriverse" are "destined to disappear, losing a 'whole part of reality' to ontological oblivion," as is illustrated by "a novel [about] the disappearance of orangutans" (167). Ellmann's narrative underlines that the vanishing of animal perspectives threatens cross-species worlds, too, for without cougars there will be no more surprising partnerships with dogs, or with human readers.

The cougar plot registers grief about the precarious existence of wildlife via references to bad zoos and blind violence toward creatures with minds and families of their own. Yet it nurtures hope, too, as this storyline follows an optimistic arc, establishes heartening ties between the lion and other oppressed groups, and features a surprisingly peaceful predator. Because it centers on a mountain lion in Ohio, first of all, the novel latches on to debates about the so-called Eastern Cougar, a subspecies that has been declared extinct but remains the subject of feverish speculation. These debates are referenced in several passages, which I list in sequence to clarify the arc of this story about a supposedly extinct creature:

> the fact that there used to be cougars in Ohio, and now they're thinking of allowing them *back* because there are too many deer, . . . originally they killed all the cougars off because they didn't want them eating the deer, . . . go figure, . . . I guess it's too late now just to leave the ecosystem to fend for itself, since we've destroyed most of it . . . (Ellmann 2019a: 269)

> I don't think this lion *could* be an Eastern Cougar, . . . they're not "endangered," they're just gone, . . . they've been pushed out of [river valleys] by people, so now they have to live in "attics," meaning mountains, deserts and swamps, . . . I guess they're called that because people don't spend much time there, just throw all their old junk in . . . (744)

> the fact that they're doing genetic tests on her . . . because if she *is* an Eastern Cougar, she must be one of the last, . . . now maybe the zoo can breed from her and . . . they can repopulate the northeast with Eastern Cougars [if they] mate her with some western cougars . . . (944–45)

Corroborating this optimistic ending, the map included in the novel (999) locates the cougar's original den in the eastern United States. The novel incites hope via historical allusions, too, for the animal is associated with Ohio's original inhabitants and the ancient earthworks that dot the landscape; "The tracker guy found the lioness at Alligator Mound . . . along with her dog companion" (942) and he named her "*Mishipeshu*, an Ojibwe word for underwater panther, I think because of her weird rain-dance in the storm" (944). As the housewife often praises the sustainable living practices of Native American societies, "Mishipeshu" appears to form a direct link with an earlier, ecologically healthier state of the United States. Via her nickname, the lioness is also affiliated with two characters with a mixed background: the tracker, who has Cherokee roots but "was brought up Italian" (924), and Stacy, who appears to "sho[w] no interest in her Indian heritage" (542), though she "got called a 'squaw' once" (585) and musicals make her feel "not white" (786). It is no coincidence that these figures are among the most positive characters of the novel, and Stacy especially represents a hopeful future; in successfully fighting off the family stalker, she reminds the mother of the female Cheyenne warrior Mocchi (782, 979), and Stacy regularly condemns the mother's ecological compromises and passive political stance, referencing the Dakota Access Pipeline protests, for example (333). The cougar activates another hopeful form of multidirectional memory as well, for a plan of her journey "looks like maps of the Underground Railroad" (945). While this creature is hunted by an organization that calls to mind the Ku Klux Klan (KKK), the FFF, her plot hence reminds readers of past social justice projects and forms of political resistance (see fig. 1). What is more, her behavior takes the form of a fugitivity and tenacity that runs parallel to Bennett's argument about the neglected uplifting connotations of animal imagery in African American writing. Time and again, the lioness slinks away "unseen" (787) and proves that she is "good at keeping out of sight" (945), like the rats and other animal "escape artists" revalorized by Bennett (2020: 50).

Ellmann's portrait of a fugitive cougar is also compatible with research on cougar-human entanglements. As Collard (2012b: 38) points out, work in animal ethics privileges intimate encounters, despite the fact that "face-to-face encounters with humans are neither desirable nor possible" for multiple species including mountain lions and "emphases on the spatial requirements of animals are necessary to rein in the invasive actions that may be generated by the . . . [human] pursuit of encounters [with wild animals]" (25). We should learn to live apart

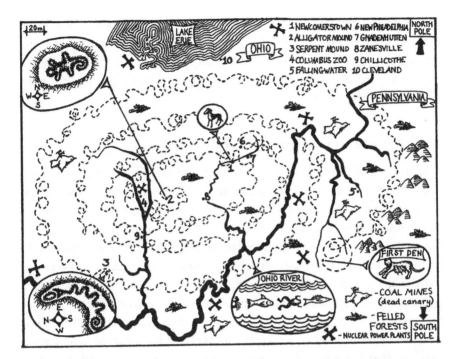

Figure 1. Mishipeshu's spiraling journey recalls "maps of the Underground Railroad."
Reproduced by permission of Lucy Ellmann.

together with such creatures, in short. *Ducks, Newburyport* offers a similar lesson. A scene with a jogger seems to have only one outcome—"The woman . . .
lay there frozen, assuming she would soon be dead for having come between a
mother cougar and her cubs" (Ellmann 2019a: 517)—but it ends without violence. The rest of the narrative underlines that the cougar behaves surprisingly
peacefully; she is a "wrathful mother without her cubs" (591), yet she becomes
a "*folk hero*, because she never kills anybody and . . . always eludes her captors"
(897) and "considering how close she was to well-populated areas during this
journey of hers, it's incredible she wasn't spotted more [and] caused *no harm*"
(945). Apparently, humans and cougars can both flourish, as long as these fugitive
creatures are left alone. Indeed, the cougar family initially gets into trouble, not
because of cougar haters but because two "nature lovers" come across the cubs
and assume that these cute "baby animals" have been abandoned, turning this
dramatic event into a misguided tale of human kindness, ironically (617). The
novel also abruptly breaks off before the two storylines and families meet in the

zoo, as if to suggest that imaginative encounters trump physical ones. We should privilege narrative instead of physical contact with wildlife, it seems, and reimagine the cultural meaning of the cougar in a way that foregrounds its tenacity and fugitivity—and provides conceptual resources to women exposed to violence, like Stacy and her mother.

5. Audrey and Gracia, Overworked Chickens

Ellmann's novel deploys the subplots of Jim and Mishipeshu to ponder cross-species sympathy and teamwork and the threat of extinction alongside the promise of fugitivity. This section studies a final character (or group of characters) that appears throughout the novel, even more frequently than the cougar, yet remains in the background even more than the eagles. I am thinking of the novel's numerous chickens, which take the form of anonymized animals but also named individuals such as Audrey and Gracia. Because these latter figures are hard to perceive, we should tweak Woloch's argument slightly and differentiate between "minor minor characters" (2003: 228) and "'tertiary' characters" (229). While a human figure like Ronny seems peripheral at first but turns out to be a major minor character, uncharismatic animal figures can be much harder to identify than even minor minor characters. Developing Woloch's remarks about servants and Kreilkamp's insights about animals, I accordingly propose that we reserve the term "tertiary characters" for these doubly obscured figures—and it is no coincidence, we will see, that both chickens and servants blend even more into the background. Ellmann's chickens deserve our attention for at least three reasons. First, they are the novel's primary example of creatures who are exploited in the service of industrial food production. Like the other animals, second, these chickens shed light on the narrative's human figures, their zany regime of neoliberal labor especially. Finally, the housewife's reflections on the family chickens again trace the outlines of their mental worlds and delineate a collaborative form of multispecies work that recalls the partnership between Jim and Mishipeshu.

The novel's subplots involving pet dogs and wild cougars reveal both systemic violence and cautious hope, and the same is true of chickens. Throughout *Ducks, Newburyport*, the mother ponders the horrors of factory farming and the destructive nature of modern food production. This deep-seated unease about farms is a logical consequence of her worries about food preparation and pie production. She sighs that "I don't even think I *like* meat anymore, . . . livestock farming doesn't have to be this bad" (Ellmann 2019a: 520–21) and "the way they treat newborn chicks on factory farms makes me feel like throwing up, . . . we *gotta* stop eating chicken, . . . maybe we should all become vegetarians" (735). Nor can the problem be restricted to meat: "Mother cows run mooing after the trucks carrying their calves away, . . . all so I can make all these dumb *pies*, . . . there's so much milk around now, they don't even know what to do with it" (559). An important ingredient in this unease is the structural link between meat, violence, and gender. As Carol Adams ([1990] 2019: 178) memorably puts it in her groundbreaking account of "the sexual politics of meat," "we are continuously eating mothers." Most women are now on hormone replacement therapy pills, Ellmann's (2019a: 616) housewife muses, and "they'll be giving that stuff to . . . chickens too, to keep them laying." We also hear about a murderer who started killing "because of an argument . . . with his *girlfriend*" and was spotted eating "a big steak, [and] enjoying his dinner too, . . . smacking his lips and talking . . . while he chewed" (769) before finally being arrested while eating "a lot of McNuggets" (822). These observations are traced back to their source in a particularly grim anecdote:

> The name keeps changing, but not the practices . . . at the egg factory . . . , the fact that the guy who started it all had already been convicted of animal cruelty . . . I've seen the pictures . . . millions upon millions of white chickens, crammed into three-tiered "coops" that looked like Auschwitz, . . . there were *sixty-four* of those buildings and each one held 85,000 laying hens, the fact that treating farm animals like that just seems so *ungrateful*, Make America Grateful Again, . . . the fact that after the tornadoes, . . . there were millions of dead and injured white chickens . . . but not all of them were *dead* [and] they just left them all . . . to rot and peck at each other until they all died . . . the fact that the chicken factory used slave labor too, undocumented, underage Guatamalans, *child slaves*, . . . I feel like . . . giving them a piece of my mind, speaking as a mom *and* a poultry farmer . . . , the fact that . . . they were still allowed to keep dumping manure into the creek, killing off all the fish for fifteen miles downstream . . . (392–93, 404)

Though the mother criticizes these industrial farms, her experiences teach that this system is hard to abandon. Stacy is "going all vegan" (345) and the mother objects to the children eating KFC because she does not "like their standards on animal welfare" (586). Yet Stacy grabs "the last piece" of bacon at one point (250), and the mother finally caves and "the kids ate about five hundred drumsticks each" (592). Factory farms implicate sundry creatures—like hogs, who "don't deserve to be made into bacon, but everybody likes bacon so much" (26)—but chickens occupy a special, unenviable place in this respect. When the family discusses global warming, the mother comments that "chickens are the one thing that *will* be kept going, whatever happens, because people *have* to have their fried chicken" (599). As these passages show, the novel unveils the brutality of factory farms while hinting at the inconsistencies of modern consumer behavior.

In calling attention to these horrible practices, *Ducks, Newburyport* puts the question of animal abuse on the agenda but also the question of alienated labor. Chickens and pigs deserve a better life, but these Guatemalan child slaves and most workers of the neoliberal economy do, too. Bearing in mind the previous sections, it appears that the mother is not just shy like Jim and threatened by gun-crazy men like the cougar but also overworked like these chickens. This exhaustion is due to the fact that she runs a cake business: "I was running a *charity* pie service there for a while, because I'd never considered the *actual* costs" (182). But it is also caused by her innumerable tasks as a mother of four: "My entire life is now spent catering to their needs . . . , cleaning toilets, filling lunchboxes, . . . then there's all the dusting, sweeping, ironing, making beds, washing sheets, . . . fielding the phone calls, planning the meals, . . . and then of course, in my spare time, baking a million pies" (18–19). She is not the only mother distracted by repetitive chores, for her situation confirms a well-known but persistent structural imbalance in terms of the domestic division of labor, as she points out herself: "French women do twenty-five times as much housework as men, and Canadian women do five times as much" (247). As a result of this situation, the mother's monologue is replete with lists, verbs, and lists of verbs: "If you work at home you're doing a million different things at once, making beds and washing clothes and gardening and . . . ironing and feeding chickens" (609). One implication of the narrator's zany regime is that the novel constitutes a performative paradox in the sense that Ellmann's protagonist does not have much time for hobbies like reading (despite her desire to relax with an Anne Tyler) and would be incapable of writing *Ducks, Newburyport*, even though the novel implies that her thoughts are worth recording in full, granular detail.

The notion of the zany is instructive here, as it illuminates the activities of the narrator and several other characters, including her chickens. As Sianne Ngai explains in *Our Aesthetic Categories* (2012), the zany is a productive category (ironically) for thinking about modern art, labor, and gender. The term refers to a specific type of behavior: "comically strenuous efforts" (175) with "a stressed-out, even desperate quality" (185). This frenetic behavior can be retraced to a stock figure from the commedia dell'arte, meaning that the term originally designates "the style of a kind of person defined by a specifically nonspecific kind of work: personal services provided in the household" (194). As Ngai documents, however, the term's meaning has shifted because this type of reproductive labor first became associated with women and was subsequently generalized in postindustrial economies, meaning that male labor has become feminized and precarious, too. The "zany" does not simply name a mode of stressed-out activity, in other words, but the often unpaid service labor of homemakers in particular—a mode of work that has migrated to the rest of the economy without diminishing the claims such work continue to make on women's private lives or improving its public prestige. What makes Ngai's argument even more pertinent here is that the zany is associated with a certain style of writing, which "bristle[s] with markers of affective insistence: italics, dashes, exclamation points, full capitals" (184) and captures "the experience of an agent confronted by . . . too many things coming at her at once," as in "a Thomas Pynchon novel, [which] bombard[s] protagonist and reader with hundreds of informational bits" (183). These observations accord with *Ducks, Newburyport* in terms of style and content, given the novel's lists, italics, and data overload. As Ellmann's (2019a: 912) narrator aptly formulates it, she keeps "ricocheting off one horror after another like a Spinning Jenny." While the narrator's life and language exemplify a zany aesthetic, the same is true of the novel's other characters, including its many professors. But animals are no exception; "Fewer than ten percent of Americans now work in factories or on farms, . . . only *chickens* work in factories now" (311) and "they've even figured out how to overwork *bees* now" (521).

Ducks, Newburyport indicates that chickens and other gendered animals are brutally reduced to food and that their overworked lives resemble those of human laborers and homemakers. But the novel features individualized chickens, too, who experience the world in unique ways and star in yet another subplot for readers attentive to these tertiary characters. The housewife hypothesizes at one point that "the chickens can't decide whether to go in or come out" (789) and when the cougar stalks the garden they remain silent, "sensing danger" (886). In fact, the mother notes, "I'm sure even *chickens* worry about stuff, . . . the fact that hens pant and squawk while laying eggs, . . . it's a big effort for birds to lay eggs, but nobody ever thinks about that, nobody but poultry farmers . . . and maybe vegans" (511–12). In another illustration of this focus on animal worlds, parenthetically, the novel invites us to see battery hen factories through the eyes of a bee, as it were: "It must be hard for a bee to pass a thing like that, but some bees must have to fly past there now and then" (389). As the mother's caring stance toward the family chickens implies, her backyard coop is presented as an alternative to the factory farm, recalling Despret's (2016: 181) remarks about the usually invisible "collaborative work" between small-scale farmers and their animals and the joint mental worlds that result "when farmers and animals are happy, together" (167). Ellmann's (2019a: 310–12) protagonist reflects on this stressful but hopeful cohabitation as follows:

> Having hens is worrisome . . . , they've gotta be let out early in the morning [and] checked midday . . . and locked back up in the coop at sundown, the fact that at least we don't have a rooster, . . . I couldn't *resist* keeping [Nebuchadnezzar] because he was so good-looking, but then he started attacking the chickens, the cats, and *me*, . . . they need tending even in a blizzard, and it's all up to me, the fact that not everybody realizes the pecking order involves actual pecking, . . . it may not be the most democratic-looking form of government but it seems to work, . . . the fact that Audrey's currently top hen, . . . she's so nice and fat and she runs the whole show like a queen, . . . she's very affectionate towards me now, . . . the fact that they're free range but not organic [because] you have to watch every single little thing the chickens eat if they're organic, and it's much more fun for them to . . . eat whatever they want, . . . the fact that they're not shy, . . . I think our chickens are pretty happy . . .

This situation is not devoid of violence, either between these chickens or between them and their keeper. For the housewife may again speculate about their mental worlds, but these animals are not safely individualized, seeing that the family employs "an ever-changing number of hens" (310) and the freezer contents include "the last of Nebuchadnezzar (coq au vin)" (455). Nevertheless, the housewife's chickens are shown to have names and lives of their own: "Gracia is seven years old and still laying, . . . she should get an award" (699). Though they are easily overlooked, moreover, these animals participate in the story. The chickens look "like they're sinking" (597) after the flash flood and the housewife decides to "put the poor old chickens in the basement" (988–89) after the home-jacking. Indeed, the chickens actually play a pivotal role; apart from the fact that they lure the cougar to the housewife's yard and to Jim, a joint visit to the therapist reveals that Stacy silently resents the fact that her mother "turned her playhouse into a *chicken coop*" (914), and the ending discloses that the man who delivers their chicken feed has been stalking them. The novel includes a more independent anecdote, too, which accentuates the themes of motherhood, vulnerability, and teamwork; the mother found a "wood pigeon egg" and "unlocked the coop so I could push the little egg under one of the chickens" (674), but even Gracia "couldn't hatch [it], . . . it was probably already too late" (699).

6. Coda: Good Neighbors

After profiling four animal characters from Ellmann's encyclopedic novel, and detailing their worlds, subplots, and vulnerabilities, I will conclude my analysis with the help of a last leitmotif and brief observations about the novel's position in terms of characters, modernism, and climate fiction. The previous sections have posited that one critical and characteristic feature of *Ducks, Newburyport* is that it tests the reader's attention via subplots involving humans and a copious cast of pets, wild creatures, and farm animals. Through figures like Jim, Mishipeshu, Audrey, and Gracia—and Frederick, Mr. President and the First Lady, Nebuchadnezzar, Junie, Opal, Pepito, Cecil the lion, and abundant bees, ducks, and other creatures—the narrative explores human concerns, related to the mother and Stacy especially, but it also integrates anecdotes about other lives at a time when the harmful domestication of the planet is an urgent problem. On a structural level, the novel's animals occupy divergent slots in its elaborate character system, ranging from coprotagonists and major minor characters to near-invisible tertiary figures. Accordingly, Ellmann's novel presents its readers with a cross-species narrative about "the mom vs. the many," which both rewards critical scrutiny and deserves creative imitation. Or, given the novel's emphasis on cross-species cooperation, it might be more accurate to speak of "the mom *and* the many."

Bearing in mind these remarks, we should now return to the text's status as an example of cli-fi and metamodernism. As many commentators have noted, most climate narratives adopt conventional literary strategies that implicitly endorse the centrality of human agency. Given the limitations of this myopic approach in the Anthropocene, Adeline Johns-Putra (2018: 27) insists that we should explore the "postmodern turn in climate change fiction," in which novels target "realist, imperialist, and anthropocentric" views (33) via a critique of "perspectival singularity" (31) and a focus on powerful "quiet heroine[s]" (39). We have found something similar in Ellmann's version of the "everyday Anthropocene," seeing that *Ducks, Newburyport* criticizes colonial violence and promotes female perspectives—while broadening the scope of domestic fiction so as to include other, often gendered animals. Yet its epic interior monologue signals that Ellmann aligns herself with a modernist rather than postmodernist legacy. That choice can be clarified by unpacking a recent argument by Cary Wolfe. Responding to the apparent obsolescence of animal studies at a time when cultural scholars are turning to geology, Wolfe (2020: 132) proclaims that "the discourse of Gaia and the Anthropocene . . . has abandoned 'the question of the animal' prematurely, because what the site of 'the Animal' shows is that Flat Ontologies . . . evacuate the radical discontinuity between . . . living vs. physical systems." We should not conflate objects like rocks and animals like cougars, he contends, because living systems are composed of organisms that construct distinct *Umwelten*, and the resulting behaviors and interactions are more unpredictable than and irreducible to mechanical forms of causation. In worrying about the world, we should not lose sight of the fact that it is composed of manifold *worlds* produced and inhabited by heterogeneous life forms, and novels about unfamiliar creatures and their vantage points can help to keep in mind this difference between geology and biology, which is worth underlining at a time of species extinctions and widespread human violence. This point about cross-species perspectivism is a typically if not exclusively modernist concern, and it hence elucidates why a metamodernist version of climate fiction forms an effective response to the call for more imaginative stories about planetary upheaval.

In mapping the nonhuman worlds of characters like Jim, Mishipeshu, Audrey, and Gracia, *Ducks, Newburyport* stresses that their lives are relegated to the sidelines, integrated into human projects, and exposed to brutal violence. But we have noticed that the text counterbalances the anxiety of perspectival obliteration with the hope of multispecies teamwork. The novel's ultimate response to that ambivalent condition can be summarized with the help of a final leitmotif, that of the neighbor. Ellmann's (2019a: 419) protagonist admits that they hardly know their neighbors, including the Kinkel family, meaning that a lesson from L. M. Montgomery's books does not apply: "She thinks you can solve any neighbor problem just by bringing over a cake." In yet another reference to a female writer, she observes how, in the *Little House on the Prairie* series, Laura Ingalls Wilder "writes as if there were no other people for miles around, . . . the fact that they probably didn't see Indians as neighbors" (542). The mother also stresses that "it's not very neighborly" of companies like DuPont to poison the environment (929) and explains that the full name of the family stalker is Ronald Neighbor, an illustration of the ironic fact "that most of the first European inhabitants here were called Neighbour" (928). Nevertheless, she rejects the survivalist outlook of preppers because she would trust "neighbors and friends" in an apocalyptic scenario (605). And in fact, after the housewife and her children manage to subdue Ronny, in a satisfying rebuke to systemic masculine violence that makes good use of the laundry pile (969–72), the reader learns that she was wrong about the

Kinkels, who turn out to be "good neighbors" (973). So one lesson we might glean from this wide-ranging novel is that we should attempt to behave in a more hospitable fashion and acknowledge forms of life that are adjacent as well as surprising and fugitive. It models for us how we can treat everyone as neighbors instead of sitting ducks, including the chickens in our coops, the dogs (and trees) in our gardens, and the remaining critters of our polluted, fragmented wilderness: "Sometimes it seems like plants and animals live in an alternative universe from us, . . . or they're all in a nature film or something, but actually they're right here *with* us" (527).

Ben De Bruyn teaches English literature at UCLouvain, Belgium. He is the author of *The Novel and the Multispecies Soundscape* (2020) and coeditor of *Planetary Memory in Contemporary American Fiction* (2018) and *Literature Now* (2016). He has also published several articles on climate fiction and animal narratives in journals such as *Studies in the Novel* and the *Oxford Literary Review*.

Works Cited

Adams, Carol J. (1990) 2019. *The Sexual Politics of Meat: A Feminist-Vegetarian Critical Theory.* London: Bloomsbury.

Bennett, Joshua. 2020. *Being Property Once Myself: Blackness and the Ends of Man.* Cambridge, MA: Harvard University Press.

Brooks, Peter. 2020. *Balzac's Lives.* New York: New York Review Books.

Callaway, Elizabeth. 2018. "Seeing What's Right in Front of Us: *The Bone Clocks*, Climate Change, and Human Attention." *Humanities* 7, no. 11: 1–12.

Collard, Rosemary-Claire. 2012a. "Cougar Figures, Gender, and the Performances of Predation." *Gender, Place, and Culture* 19, no. 4: 518–40.

Collard, Rosemary-Claire. 2012b. "Cougar-Human Entanglements and the Biopolitical Un/Making of Safe Space." *Environment and Planning D: Society and Space* 30, no. 1: 23–42.

Despret, Vinciane. (2012) 2016. *What Would Animals Say If We Asked the Right Questions?* Translated by Brett Buchanan. Minneapolis: Minnesota University Press.

Ellmann, Lucy. 2019a. *Ducks, Newburyport.* Cornwall: Galley Beggar.

Ellmann, Lucy. 2019b. "Lucy Ellman: 'We Need to Raise the Level of Discourse.'" Interview by Sian Cain. *Guardian*, September 7. www.theguardian.com/books /2019/dec/07/lucy-ellmann-ducks-newburyport-interview.

Ercolino, Stefano. 2014. *The Maximalist Novel: From Thomas Pynchon's "Gravity's Rainbow" to Roberto Bolaño's "2666."* Translated by Albert Sbragia. London: Bloomsbury.

Fraiman, Susan. 2012. "Pussy Panic versus Liking Animals: Tracking Gender in Animal Studies." *Critical Inquiry* 39, no. 1: 89–115.

Heise, Ursula. 2016. *Imagining Extinction: The Cultural Meanings of Endangered Species*. Chicago: University of Chicago Press.

Herman, David. 2018. *Narratology beyond the Human: Storytelling and Animal Life*. Oxford: Oxford University Press.

Houser, Heather. 2020. *Infowhelm: Environmental Art and Literature in an Age of Data*. New York: Columbia University Press.

James, David, and Urmila Seshagiri. 2014. "Metamodernism: Narratives of Continuity and Revolution." *PMLA* 129, no. 1: 87–100.

Johns-Putra, Adeline. 2018. "The Rest Is Silence: Postmodern and Postcolonial Possibilities in Climate Change Fiction." *Studies in the Novel* 50, no. 1: 26–42.

Kreilkamp, Ivan. 2018. *Minor Creatures: Persons, Animals, and the Victorian Novel*. Chicago: University of Chicago Press.

LeMenager, Stephanie. 2017. "Climate Change and the Struggle for Genre." In *Anthropocene Reading: Literary History in Geologic Times*, edited by Tobias Menely and Jesse Oak Taylor, 220–38. University Park: Penn State University Press.

Letzler, David. 2012. "Encyclopedic Novels and the Cruft of Fiction." *Studies in the Novel* 44, no. 3: 304–24.

Ngai, Sianne. 2012. *Our Aesthetic Categories: Zany, Cute, Interesting*. Cambridge, MA: Harvard University Press.

Nixon, Rob. 2011. *Slow Violence and the Environmentalism of the Poor*. Cambridge, MA: Harvard University Press.

Wolfe, Cary. 2020. "What 'the Animal' Can Teach 'the Anthropocene.'" *Angelaki* 25, no. 3: 131–45.

Woloch, Alex. 2003. *The One vs. the Many: Minor Characters and the Space of the Protagonist in the Novel*. Princeton, NJ: Princeton University Press.

Review Essay

SAMUEL FALLON

Amanda Anderson, Rita Felski, and Toril Moi,
Character: Three Inquiries in Literary Studies,
Chicago: University of Chicago Press, 2019.

Aaron Kunin, *Character as Form*, London: Bloomsbury, 2019.

Characters are strange things. They are not persons, not exactly. They belong to the page, the stage, the screen, and it is central to our experience of them that we know they are fictions. Yet we feel for them nonetheless: we sympathize with them, root and fear for them, and get annoyed by them, too. When Hamlet pondered the player—"What's Hecuba to him, or he to Hecuba?"—this was the paradox that left him mystified: how is it that an imagined person can generate real and potent feelings? In *Astrophil and Stella*, written some years before *Hamlet*, Philip Sidney explored the same riddle. The forty-fifth sonnet in the sequence begins with a familiar lover's lament: although Stella sees his suffering, Astrophil complains, she "cannot skill to pity" him. Stella is not utterly impassive, however: when she hears a tragic fable of "lovers never known," Astrophil reports, pity moves her instantly to tears. For Hamlet, the surprise is that we can care about fictional people much as we care about real ones; for Astrophil, it is that sometimes we care about fictional people more readily and more deeply. So Astrophil decides to turn himself into a fiction: "Then think, my dear, that you in me do

Genre, Vol. 54, No. 2   July 2021
DOI 10.1215/00166928-9263118   © 2021 by University of Oklahoma

read / Of lover's ruin some sad tragedy: / I am not I, pity the tale of me" (Sidney, *Astrophil and Stella*, sonnet 45). In the poem's final line, Astrophil becomes to Stella what he already is to us: a character.

Sidney's poem traces two distinct ways of thinking about characters. The first we can call the formalist position: it insists on a distinction between persons and characters, reminding us that the latter are textual artifacts, assemblages of words fashioned, as John Frow (2014: 2) has recently put it, into "person-like entities." The second we can call the realist position: it is concerned with the responses characters elicit, the feelings they provoke, the uses they invite; it reminds us that characters are *like persons* and that our relationships with them are like our relationships with people. For Sidney, there is no necessary conflict between the two views. His sonnet suggests that character is beguiling just because of its artifice and that the remove of fictionality is what makes sympathy possible. In contemporary criticism, however, the formalist and the realist approaches have come to seem like opposing camps, and character has emerged as a stage for a confrontation of competing ideas of what criticism should be—so we might suspect, at least, from the appearance of two polemical new books, each determined to put the study of character on new ground and each possessed of a very different idea about where it has been.

The first, Amanda Anderson, Rita Felski, and Toril Moi's *Character: Three Inquiries in Literary Studies*, describes a discipline still in the thrall of formalism and its injunctions against treating characters as if they were persons. Those strictures, they warn, have left us "with nothing to say about characters as objects of identification, sources of emotional response, or agents of moral vision and behavior" (4). By contrast, Aaron Kunin's *Character as Form* insists that we have hardly any other way of talking about them. "Most readers," Kunin declares early in his book, "think that the job of a character is to individuate," which is why we tend to approach them in ethical and psychological terms—as objects, that is, of identification (7). Where Anderson, Felski, and Moi want to "develop a nonformalist understanding of form" (19), Kunin's aim is to teach us, as if for the first time, how to see character *as* a form. More precisely, he wants us to see it as a device of generalization rather than individuation: "I think that a character is a collection of every example of a kind" (5). *Character* urges us to forget form in order to focus on the claims—ethical and aesthetic—that characters make on us; *Character as Form* demands that we remember it so that we can see how characters typologize the world.

Reading the two books alongside one another, one is struck by the difference not just between their critical prescriptions but between their assessments of the field: it is as if they have been reading altogether different bodies of scholarship. But a stranger conclusion quickly follows: that, despite their direct opposition, each assessment is substantially correct. It is true, as Anderson, Felski, and Moi claim, that it remains customary, perhaps obligatory, for critics to distinguish fictional from real persons. Yet it is equally true, as Kunin suggests, that the most influential recent theorists of character—from Catherine Gallagher to Alex Woloch to Blakey Vermeule—have focused on processes of individuation and modes of readerly investment. The fact that the criticism on the subject of character is susceptible to nearly opposite readings may be a measure of its syncretism, as critics draw on the resources of formalism and its alternatives at once. But the simultaneous arrival of *Character* and *Character as Form* suggests that syncretism is on the way out, and that the argument between formalism and realism—or for their compatibility—will have to be had in the open.

*

Like the other volumes in Chicago's Trios series, *Character: Three Inquiries in Literary Studies* features an essay by each of its three authors, preceded by a jointly written introduction. In Anderson, Felski, and Moi, *Character* brings together three of the most eminent literary critics working today, and their collaboration bears the stamp of each of its contributors: a grounding in ordinary language philosophy drawn from Moi's work on Ludwig Wittgenstein and Stanley Cavell; the interest in modes of attachment that Felski brought to the center of the discipline in *The Limits of Critique* (2015); and the attention to ethos that has motivated much of Anderson's writing. Their different modes of argument complement each other as well: in moving from Moi's ground-clearing polemic to Felski's typologizing to Anderson's close reading, the book gradually turns from theory (or rather, as we shall see, *anti*theory) to practice—first calling for a criticism that takes seriously the "claims [characters] make on their readers" then showing us what such a criticism would look like (3).

Moi's essay, the first and most essential, confronts the volume's primary bogey: "the taboo," as she calls it, "on treating characters as if they are real" (29). In Moi's telling, this taboo has two central problems. The first is that it misrecognizes how people actually experience characters. Yes, we can love them or fear for them or be compelled by them, but we are never under the illusion that characters are actually people; even children quickly learn the difference between fact and fiction. The second problem is that because it imagines the confusion of characters and persons to be far more widespread than it is, the taboo needlessly restricts how we talk about characters. Ordinary readers may speculate about the inner lives of characters, and they may imagine their prehistories or further adventures, but critics will see only a category error, a failure to observe the difference between life and art. Moi traces this prejudice to its apparent origin: the archly titled pamphlet *How Many Children Hath Lady Macbeth?*, published in 1933 by L. C. Knights, then a doctoral student at Cambridge and an acolyte of F. R. Leavis. For Knights, character was an interpretive red herring, an "abstraction" that effaces the formal "pattern" of a text and the "total response" to it. Moi makes quick work of Knights's argument: how, she asks, can "total response" be any less an abstraction than character or plot? But Moi also historicizes it. Knights's polemic, she shows, was an act of professional self-assertion, undertaken against an older generation of belletristic amateurs and one of aesthetic position-taking, championing highbrow modernism against old-fashioned realism. The intervention came at a decisive moment in the history of literary study, when formalism became the methodological banner of a professionalizing discipline.

Contemporary critics don't have the same excuse. For us, Moi suggests, polemical edge has softened into *doxa*, and a refusal to read characters as anything but forms has mired character criticism in a series of pseudoproblems. Thus, she argues, when John Frow describes characters as "ontologically hybrid beings" (1)—at once persons and textual constructs—he is finding paradox where none need be: readers have no problem talking about characters as though they are people, despite knowing full well that they aren't. The suggestion of logical incoherence or doubleness arises only out of a determination to give a formal account of what characters are. Moi has no interest in developing such a theory of character; instead, she urges critics to remember the range of ordinary responses that they have trained themselves to forget. What are characters? The answer, Moi writes, will come "not in speculation, but in an examination of use—that is, in how we talk about characters" (60).

The second essay, Felski's, is a natural companion to Moi's, for it offers a taxonomy of the various modes of character use loosely gathered under the label of "identification." Identification is a promising and a difficult category, at once formal, phenomenological, and ethical in its force, and the great value of Felski's approach is its careful delineation of these tendencies. She adduces five modes of identification: *alignment*, or the formal framing of perspective; *allegiance*, as ethical or aesthetic commitment; *recognition*, in the sense of coming to know; *empathy*, as feeling with or feeling for; and—the most provocative—*ironic identification*, in which estrangement serves as the paradoxical glue between character and reader. These are productive distinctions, and they suggest the power of a sustained focus on response and attachment. Yet this approach may not be as new as Felski, like Moi, thinks it is. Hans Robert Jauss offered a strikingly similar taxonomy of identification some decades earlier—his categories of associative, admiring, and sympathetic identification are, in fact, near matches for Felski's alignment, allegiance, and empathy—but Felski addresses Jauss only to distinguish his definition of ironic identification from her own (see Jauss 1982a: 152–88). Like his fellow reader response theorist Wolfgang Iser, Jauss is mostly overlooked in *Character*, as if the book's insistence on the unbroken dominance of formalism, and hence on its own novelty, requires that precedents be forgotten.

The last essay in *Character* is Anderson's perceptive study of rumination— the slow, directionless circling of experience in the mind—in Eliot, Trollope, and Woolf. The essay's patient readings practice the sort of criticism that Moi and Felski call for, considering examples of ruminative thought in order to show the special capacity of novelistic character to depict the "phenomenology of the thinking life" and the gravity of moral experience (131). More precisely, the capacity of *realist* character: if Anderson's method bears out Moi's and Felski's prescriptions, her examples, drawn from Eliot, Trollope, and Woolf, realize the aesthetic commitments that guide Moi's critical prescriptions. In her earlier book, *Ibsen and the Birth of Modernism*, Moi (2006: 19) took aim at what she called, following Fredric Jameson, the "ideology of modernism," claiming that it had distorted literary history and criticism alike. Realism and formalism, she argues, both emerged as branches of modernism—they were linked as skeptical responses to idealism—but as formalism became modernism's default mode, it began to enforce a vocabulary rooted in autonomy, reflexivity, and irony. Critics in the grip of the ideology of modernism had no way of appreciating Ibsen's realism, just as today—as Moi argues in an essay adapted from *Character* for the magazine *The Point*—they lack a language for the neorealist "existential turn" in the autofiction of Knausgaard, Cusk, Heti, and Ferrante: the formalist preference for irony and detachment, she suggests, is helpless in the face of the moral seriousness that realism demands (Moi 2020: 54–59). Such seriousness is what Anderson's readings aim for, their subtle appraisals of depictions of thinking bringing out the realism at the heart of even the high modernist Woolf.

Character's preference for realism is one reason why Frow—whose examples favor modernism and postmodernism—comes in for sharp criticism. His emphasis on the "ontological hybridity" of character, Moi argues, traps criticism in the arid air of theoretical classification; worse, it mystifies the ordinary ways that we use and respond to the characters we meet. But hybridity is hard to banish. Felski writes in her essay of "the two-foldedness of character—as both person and aesthetic device" (92); the modes of identification she traces remind us that characters "are portmanteau creatures," "Janus-faced figures" (90, 119). It is not that she is backsliding into metaphysics but rather that use—when one really follows it—can't help but implicate the modes of irony and reflexivity that formalism prizes.

*

Frow is, in any case, an imperfect antagonist: too much a syncretist, too willing to balance form with attention to response and attachment. In *Character as Form*, Aaron Kunin provides a more suitable one. Kunin *is* an uncompromising formalist—so much so that he idly muses, in a characteristically eccentric aside, whether Frances Ferguson is "the only true formalist critic" (16). His idea of form is Ferguson's—it is what "makes it possible for there to be 'more than one of something'"—and even critics who call themselves formalists, he suggests, tend to fall short of this degree of abstraction: we are caught up in describing aspects of experience, or of style (16). Style, Kunin writes, is what attaches to particular artworks or to individual persons, as a qualitative relation among parts; form, by contrast, transcends particular instances, as an iterative principle of composition. The articulation of this distinction occupies nearly the whole of the introduction to *Character as Form*, a puzzling choice until one sees that the point is to justify the austerity of the book's account of character. For Kunin, character has nothing to do with personhood; it is a form in the strong sense: a device of collection, iteration, and generalization.

The roots of this conception of character lie not in the realist novel—the privileged genre of *Character*—but in the Theophrastan character books that flourished in England and France in the seventeenth century. A student of Aristotle, Theophrastus wrote his *Characters* as a survey of thirty moral types in fourth-century Athens. The Theophrastan mode—as found in the sketches of Joseph Hall, Thomas Overbury, John Earle, and Jean de La Bruyère, as well as the drama of Jonson and Molière—asked its readers to imagine characters as kinds. When Earle sketches the figure of the Gallant, for instance, he doesn't give us a particular gallant but a personified compendium of the sorts of things that gallants do; his Gallant is every gallant in one. Kunin's gambit is to turn this mode of character writing—a historically specific and in many respects idiosyncratic one—into a more general theory of character. It is a striking and arguably a perverse project, reading Renaissance character forward, but no more perverse than the more familiar one of reading novelistic character backward. "I take seriously the idealism of characteristic writing," he writes, "in order to rewrite subsequent literary history and include everything we call a character in the same way that the realist concept of character rewrites earlier literary history so that what used to be called character has to be renamed caricature or stereotype" (45).

The result is a highly original book and a strange one—often compelling, sometimes brilliant, occasionally frustrating. Kunin's prose is direct and conversational, capable of aphoristic pith, yet his arguments wander and circle, working in and out of readings of an eclectic range of texts and films. The first chapter, "Many Is Not More Than One," is a case in point: it moves through *The Merchant of Venice*, *Our Mutual Friend*, Milton's companion poems "L'Allegro" and "Il Penseroso," *Bridget Jones's Diary*, the Marx Brothers' *Monkey Business*, Doug Allen's comic strip *Steven*, and the Korean film *Yeopgi Girl* in order to unfold Kunin's idea of character as "a device that collects every example of a kind" (38). It is in this chapter, too, that Kunin weighs up the critical literature on character. Seeing character as a device of collection, he suggests, means letting go of theories (such as Alex Woloch's [2004: 13] account of "character-space") that contain characters within texts: a central function of character is to generalize across them. But it doesn't mean embracing approaches that focus on the movement of characters between texts: collection is distinct from David Brewer's (2005: 78) concept of "character migration," Kunin writes, because it depends on a logic not of influence but of abstraction. What links Woloch and Brewer, along with most other critics of character, Kunin suggests, is the mistake of conceiving of character by analogy to personhood. Characters and persons, he argues, instead should be seen as reflecting dialectically opposed logics, the former framed by a principle of "abundance" (they are types that can be exemplified by many different individuals) and the latter by a principle of "transformation" (each can enact many different characters). This is why Kunin tends toward examples like Dickens's eccentric Mr. Boffin, who accumulates books about misers, building an archive of miserliness even as he learns to play the miser himself.

Yet even Boffin suggests the difficulty of sustaining these distinctions. He is a collector, an abundant gatherer of instances, but he is also himself an instance: he acts the part of miser, but only in order to set up his eventual transformation into another role entirely, that of the loving uncle. There are things that Boffin does, in short, that we will have a hard time describing without a framework of personal agency. But there is another reason to hesitate. It may strike us that an example like Boffin's obsessive book buying invites the sort of confusion that Kunin warns of in his introduction—the confusion, that is, of style for form, of a representation of collecting for the structural principle of collection.

The latter chapters of *Character as Form* repeatedly court this confusion, converting the form of character into styles of subjectivity. The second chapter, "Banish the World," finds the paradigmatic case of Kunin's definition of character in the figure of the misanthrope. "The paradox at the heart of misanthropy," he writes, "is to be in the world and not in the world," and character, too, wants to escape from the world it sorts and classifies (91). After all, the process of collection produces curiously antisocial communities: the misers that Boffin collects have nothing to do with each other except for their being alike. "A character forms a community," Kunin writes, "by associating without relating examples," and misanthropy turns this refusal of relation into a way of life (106). In the fourth chapter, the misanthropic banishment of the world takes a more extreme form: the wish to be an object. The precipitate of Kunin's stringent formalism is a fascination with withdrawal—into a solitude unburdened by human relations, an idealism that can weigh up the world from without—though in truth it is hard to say which comes first, method or mood. It is no wonder, in either case, that Kunin has little time for the relations of attachment, identification, and response to which Moi, Felski, and Anderson direct us: "I am not interested in what readers do with characters" (56). A criticism of use keeps us in the world, he suggests, but the point of art is to take us elsewhere.

Kunin's formalism thus encodes an idealism that is calibrated to oppose just the sort of realism favored, as a matter of aesthetic commitment and critical practice, by the authors of *Character*. To be clear, Kunin seems as unaware of *Character* as Moi, Felski, and Anderson are of *Character as Form*. So it is a remarkable coincidence that, at the heart of his discussion of the relation between idealism and realism, Moi turns up as his opponent. The passage, which appears in the third chapter, "What Fiction Means," mounts an argument against Moi's case for realism in *Ibsen and the Birth of Modernism*. Idealism for Moi was an ideological and aesthetic constraint, and the achievement of the realists, especially Ibsen, was to escape from it, to open art to ordinary life and a nonidealized world. Kunin objects not to this historical argument but to its normative implication: that art should favor the ordinary, the concrete, the particular. "Moi does a disservice to modern artists," he writes, "insofar as she cuts them off not just from a conventional set of values but from a capacity to generalize that is a crucial source of aesthetic value" (145). We can't jettison idealism, that is, because art's relation to the world is necessarily an ideal one: art construes what it represents, presents it under a certain generalizable aspect, and so opens onto the possibility of evaluation. For Moi, aesthetic value comes from the escape of the real from the ideal; for Kunin, it arises in the ideal's apprehension of the real. This is why Kunin treats character as a complex mode of figuration—a synecdoche by which "one example of a kind includes the complete collection of examples" (166)—and why Moi insists, to the contrary, that it is "the most ordinary thing in the world" (58).

*

Moi borrows her provocation from Wittgenstein, whose influence, along with Cavell's, presides over her essay. "One person might say 'A proposition is the most ordinary thing in the world,'" Wittgenstein (1989: §93) writes in the *Philosophical Investigations*, "and another: 'A proposition—that's something very queer!'—And the latter is unable simply to look and see how propositions really work. The forms that we use in expressing ourselves about propositions and thought stand in the way."[1] For Wittgenstein, the problem is not that it is wrong to ask what propositions are but that doing so tends to leave us beguiled by the question of their form, when what really matters is what we do with them. Formalism, Moi suggests, fails character in the same way it fails the proposition: it traps us in the riddle of ontology and prevents us from getting on with the task of describing use.

In her recent book *Revolution of the Ordinary* (2017), Moi positioned Wittgenstein against what she portrayed as a post-Saussurean consensus in literary studies, a consensus marked by an enduring investment in the division of the sign between signifier and signified. The formalist account of character, she suggests in her essay in *Character*, is a largely unrecognized expression of that investment,

---

1. It is unclear whether Wittgenstein would endorse Moi's substitution of *character* for *proposition*. Elsewhere in the *Investigations*, he warns: "Don't take it as a matter of course, but as a remarkable fact, that pictures and fictitious narratives give us pleasure, occupy our minds" (§524).

with the language of "ontological hybrids" precisely mirroring the division of the sign. And each is an invented paradox: to say that signs bind marks to meanings, or that characters make persons out of words, is to find a mystery where the ordinary speaker or reader has no trouble. Yet Kunin's book is a reminder that not all formalism is Saussurean. *Character as Form* tends not to construe character in the terms of a dyadic relation between word and person; indeed, Kunin insists that characters are not like persons at all. The formal principle of character from his point of view is synecdoche, the part that stands for the whole. And we may decide that synecdoche raises real rather than confected problems: the problem, for instance, of how we coordinate types and tokens, how we manage to see individuals as at once unique beings and instances of kinds. If it does, then granting in advance the ordinariness of characters will mean missing something about how they really work.

Against Wittgensteinian deflation, then, we might set another view of the simple and the strange. "A commodity," Marx (1980: 163) tells us, "appears at first sight an extremely obvious, trivial thing. But its analysis shows that it is a very strange thing, abounding in metaphysical subtleties and theological niceties." The difference may be in part a matter of temperament, but it is surely also a function of the object in question. Commodities, unlike propositions, need to be defamiliarized, for what is decisively important about them is the set of relations encoded in their form—in the form, that is, of exchange value, which transforms the "social relation between men themselves" into "the fantastic form of a relation between things." It is when they are thus made into social things that commodities spring to life, as if they were, like that other fabrication of the human mind, the gods: "autonomous figures endowed with a life of their own, and entering into relations both with each another and with the human race" (165). An analysis of the commodity-form is necessary in order to demystify the fetishism of commodities but also in order to grasp the operations of capital, above all the grounding of the value-form in the abstraction of distinct kinds of work into undifferentiated labor-time.

Much as Marx's attitude toward formalism differs from Wittgenstein's, his idea of form differs from Saussure's. The dyadic sign may be hermetically sealed—a relation between mark and meaning that can be conceptually separated from language-in-use—but the commodity-form is something different, an objectification of the dynamics of exchange. If the proper analogy for the hybrid form of character is the sign, then Moi's complaint will ring true: an account of what character is won't tell us what character does. But what if the better analogy is the commodity? Like value, the charisma of character arises in its implication in a system of mediation. As Jauss (1982b: 19) puts it, the "communicative character" of literature "presupposes a dialogical and . . . processlike relationship between work, audience, and new work," and it is only through this relationship that characters produce their particular effects. When we open *Our Mutual Friend*, to return to one of Kunin's examples, we are outfitted in advance with certain ways of approaching fictional persons, habits so engrained that they barely register as habits: we know that Mr. Boffin isn't historically real but that we can judge him or sympathize with him regardless; we infer, through the set of references to him in the novel, a subject—a complete personality—that exceeds them; we recognize him as an individual agent, even as we work to classify him and discern the type of person he exemplifies. These operations reflect a specific "horizon of expectations," Jauss's (1982b: 22) term for the conventions of reception, derived from the assimilation of earlier works, that any new work orients itself within and against. Boffin's writing anticipates his uptake: when his performance of the Dickensian miser turns out to be a ruse, the surprise—and the rush of restored affection—hinges on the expectations presupposed in his design. Only in exchange do commodities attain the "sublime objectivity" of value (Marx 1980: 144), and only within a system of reading and response can characters come to life.

*

In attempting to turn criticism from form to use, then, *Character* (and Moi's essay in particular) risks losing sight of their mutual articulation—of the production of new forms under the pressure of reader response and of the anticipatory embedding of response in form itself. What's more, by taking aim at a monolithic idea of form, the book risks embracing an equally monolithic conception of use, replacing a formalizing account of characters as signifying constructs with a focus on the seemingly natural tendency to talk about characters like real people. That this tendency is only *seemingly* natural—that it is as much a historical determination as any other habit of reading—is easy to forget as long as we remain in the company of realism and its inheritors. Felski, at least, perceives this problem—"Why," she asks, "do critics so often equate character with the genre of realism?" (78)—and her taxonomic account of identification does more than the volume's other essays to slip its hold. But her chapter lacks the dialectical turn of Jauss's (1982a: 153) essay on the same topic: his taxonomy encodes literary history in sedimented form, with different "interaction patterns of identification" shown to have emerged in tandem with modifications in the idea of the hero. The range of responses that character elicits, Jauss suggests, is a function of the complex historical mediation of form by use.

Because *Character* is so determined to isolate use, and *Character as Form* to isolate form, neither is quite able to grasp their mediation of each other. Yet read in combination, these sharply different books suggest what an approach attuned to it might look like. For to read Kunin's book is to realize that readers once did—and, in certain ways, still do—ask characters to do things other than individuate. A longer history of character would have to come to terms with the Theophrastan impulse to generalize and classify; it would also have to make room for the durable tradition of allegory. Writers and readers in these modes used character to gather worlds of individuals into recognizable types and to realize abstractions; for them, the burden of character was precisely the work of formalization. In the passage between allegory and realism, hybridity is a condition of reading—a condition of which character use can be purified only if realism's victory is taken to be total—and the lingering resonance of typology in figures like Mr. Boffin makes clear that character never lost its impulse to generalize. Then again, even allegory retains a grasp on the particular: when Spenser's Malbecco, distorted by jealousy, at last forgets "he was a man, and Jealousy is hight," the point is precisely the violence needed to turn a person into an idea.

The history of character is a history of the coordination of particularity and generality, individual and kind. If we look closely, indeed, we see that individuation itself relies on formal rubrics, for characters and persons alike: it happens through the types and roles we invoke in order to present ourselves to the world, or to locate others in it. Formalism dies hard because we are formalists with people, too.

Think back to Sidney's sonnet. The Petrarchan mode to which it belongs fits cleanly into neither *Character* nor *Character as Form*, offering an introspective subjectivity that eludes Theophrastan generality but also an idealism at odds with novelistic realism. Yet what the poem reveals is the unexpected root of identification, and the intensely personal feeling of pity, in an intuition of typology. Sidney refuses to tell us anything specific about the characters in the "fable" that draws Stella's tears; they are, simply, "lovers never known." And when Astrophil seeks to turn himself into a character, this generality is what he claims for himself:

"Then think, my dear, that you in me do read / Of lover's ruin some sad tragedy." Although the first impulse is to take this as a poem about fiction, Astrophil's wish is not simply to be rendered imaginary; it is also, perhaps more importantly, to be rendered generic. That loss of particularity—his dissolution into the aspect of the ruined lover—is what he hopes will turn Stella's disdain to pity. Whether or not this is its effect on her, it works on us. We identify with Astrophil when and because we can see him as a certain kind of person, playing a certain role: a person whom we might be, a role that we might play. Such surrogacy is crucial to the sonnet form, with its underdetermined personae and conventional situations: the relative emptiness of its characters is just what allows readers to insert themselves. In this genre, at least, but probably in many more, the formalizing bent of character—its capacity to collect and abstract—doesn't oppose our desire to treat characters as persons. It is what makes it possible.

Samuel Fallon is assistant professor of English at the State University of New York College at Geneseo. He is the author of *Paper Monsters: Persona and Literary Culture in Elizabethan England* (2019).

Works Cited

Brewer, David A. 2005. *The Afterlife of Character, 1726–1825*. Philadelphia: University of Pennsylvania Press.
Felski, Rita. 2015. *The Limits of Critique*. Chicago: University of Chicago Press.
Frow, John. 2014. *Character and Person*. Oxford: Oxford University Press.
Jauss, Hans Robert. 1982a. *Aesthetic Experience and Literary Hermeneutics*. Translated by Michael Shaw. Minneapolis: University of Minnesota Press.
Jauss, Hans Robert. 1982b. *Toward an Aesthetic of Reception*. Translated by Timothy Bahti. Minneapolis: University of Minnesota Press.
Marx, Karl. 1980. *Capital*, vol. 1. Translated by Ben Fowkes. London: Penguin.
Moi, Toril. 2006. *Henrik Ibsen and the Birth of Modernism: Art, Theater, Philosophy*. Oxford: Oxford University Press.
Moi, Toril. 2017. *Revolution of the Ordinary: Literary Studies After Wittgenstein, Austin, and Cavell*. Chicago: University of Chicago Press.
Moi, Toril. 2020. "Real Characters." *The Point*, no. 21: 43–59.
Wittgenstein, Ludwig. 1989. *Philosophical Investigations: The English Text of the Third Edition*. Translated by G. E. M. Anscombe. New York: Macmillan.
Woloch, Alex. 2004. *The One vs. the Many: Minor Characters and the Space of the Protagonist in the Novel*. Princeton, NJ: Princeton University Press.

Book Review

JULIANNE WERLIN

Samuel Fallon, *Paper Monsters: Persona and Literary Culture in Elizabethan England*, Philadelphia: University of Pennsylvania Press, 2019.

In the final decade of the sixteenth century, Samuel Fallon argues in *Paper Monsters: Persona and Literary Culture in Elizabethan England*, a new kind of figure came into being: the literary persona. In this elegantly written and theoretically subtle study, Fallon explains that personae were writers' alter egos and their avatars. Straddling the boundary between writer and work, a persona was at once a character within a given text and its putative author. Examples included the four figures Fallon discusses, Spenser's shepherd-poet Colin Clout, Sidney's poets Philisides and Astrophil, Thomas Nashe's satiric stand-in Pierce Penniless, and the charismatic prodigal Robert Greene, the semifictional, semiautobiographical invention of the romance writer of the same name. For a moment, personae were everywhere, giving an uncanny life to literary culture. Then they vanished.

Why did personae briefly become central to literary writing? In Fallon's account, the answer lies in the nature of the literary culture of the 1590s. The persona was a device of an era in which new norms of literature—and perhaps, indeed, the idea of the literary itself—were coming into being. Using literary personae, writers constructed, and in the same breath deconstructed, such charged oppositions as exclusivity and publicity, manuscript and print, fiction and truth, writer and reader. Perhaps most importantly, writers used personae to reimagine their

Genre, Vol. 54, No. 2   July 2021
DOI 10.1215/00166928-9263131   © 2021 by University of Oklahoma

own role at a moment when modern categories of authorship had not yet stabilized. "Philisides," contemporaries understood, both was and wasn't Philip Sidney— just as "Karl Ove Knausgaard," the authorial tag, both is and isn't Karl Ove Knausgaard. The rise of the persona is thus an episode in the long and compli- cated history of the author, marking a moment when the medieval *auctor* had become inadequate to the chaotic world of print, but the modern, proprietary author had not yet fully emerged.

Yet despite being protoauthorial figures, personae were capable of drifting away from their original writers. They were all too easy to appropriate: imitators and rivals could and did pick up where their originators left off, assuming the persona of Robert Greene in posthumous sequels to his adventures, or staging a literary encounter with Colin Clout in the course of a pastoral. As a rule, then, personae outlived their parents. It is this surprising vitality that made them "paper monsters," in the phrase of Thomas Nashe, literary creations who nevertheless seemed, Fallon observes, "to exert an agency of their own" (15). Their careers reflected, then, not only writers' acts of self-invention but the tangled history of their reception.

Fallon's study begins with a chapter on Robert Greene, arguably early mod- ern England's first celebrity author. Greene, who remained England's most popu- lar native writer of prose fiction throughout the seventeenth century (only Aesop seems to have gone into more editions) wove his own biography into his works. As a growing cachet attached to his name, he teased his readers with apparent hints of self-revelation. "Robert Greene," Fallon argues, "was increasingly a tex- tual projection," yet, at the same time, "his works were increasingly imbricated in his persona" (41). Author and work merged in a figure that became, in the marketplace of print, a valuable literary property. Too lucrative a name to lay to rest, "Robert Greene" lived on in ghostly form after the death of the real Greene. Henry Chettle, Barnabe Riche, and John Dickenson all published pamphlets in which Greene's specter appeared, eager to convey some message to the London public. In doing so, Fallon argues, they revealed that Greene's persona was an elaborate construction—the relation between an author and his public necessar- ily contained a fictional dimension. Greene's continuators exposed, that is, the fantasy "that there could be any direct, unmediated relation between writer and public" (48).

In his description of the creation and reception of "Robert Greene," Fallon is working within what is still a minor growth area in early modern research: the

history of the public sphere and its complex relationship to forms of literary publication. He is conversant with Habermas and his many exponents and amenders,
such as Michael Warner. He has clearly absorbed the work of Alexandra Halasz,
whose argument that early modern print culture was one catalyst for a new kind
of public sphere informs his own analysis of the ways in which Robert Greene
interacted with his large, anonymous readership. Yet in the end, Fallon's real
concern seems to be with a rather different object—not print culture, not the
public sphere, but what he calls, following Pierre Bourdieu, the "literary field."
Ultimately, he seeks to chart the emergence of that elusive ideal, the autonomy of
the literary, in the febrile environment of late Elizabethan culture.

This, it hardly need be said, is an ambitious goal—especially for a study as
tightly focused in time, space, and topic as *Paper Monsters*. Yet two careful and
ingenious chapters on Spenser and Sidney, or rather on Spenser's Colin Clout
and Sidney's twin alter egos Astrophil and Philisides, go some distance toward
advancing his case. Both chapters begin with Spenser and Sidney's works, before
describing how their poetic personae came to appear in the writing of others, as
participants in a pastoral landscape that hovered at the threshold of fiction and
reality.

Spenser's laureate ambitions (in Richard Helgerson's phrase) and Sidney's
idealized reception have received no shortage of scholarly attention, and Fallon is
aware that he is working within a well-researched field. But the very familiarity
of the questions he addresses demonstrates the value of his approach. Because the
persona cuts across distinctions of writer and character, it reveals how fictional
representations could influence real literary relations and vice versa. It offers a
model, that is, that moves from text to context, rather than—like the majority of
scholarship—in the opposite direction. If such a movement is counterintuitive in
one sense, in another, the idea of literary history is predicated on its possibility.
This, Fallon suggests, is what the imitators and acolytes of Spenser and Sidney
had come to understand.

The autonomy of the literary is, of course, an old topic of debate, though
the plight of literature and its scholars at present may well lend it a new urgency.
In its isolation of the persona, a figure that bridges content and context, *Paper
Monsters* sheds considerable light on the development of this idea at a pivotal
moment in its history. Yet the study's attention to the literary, which is the source
of its strength, inevitably tends to depict it as an isolated practice. Such kindred
phenomena as the theater or polemical pamphleteering—Martin Marprelate, that

unruly Puritan persona, makes a few cameos—which share at least a border with the literary field are alluded to but not analyzed. Fallon thus leaves open the question of why, at this point in history, certain writers should have begun to distinguish themselves and their works from their wider society and its political and ethical codes. The most obvious candidate for a force of change is print: but although Fallon considers the era's changing forms of textual circulation closely, he rightly insists that the history of the literary cannot simply be mapped onto the history of media.

Still, perhaps the question cannot really be answered, at least not when posed in these terms. There is, as Fallon, like Bourdieu, is well aware, a circularity in the idea of any autonomous system. Indeed, circularity is precisely the point: autonomy means that the only real definition is self-definition and that the system's rules can only be determined internally.

For all the importance of personae to the literary culture of the 1590s, they were literary figures without a real future. In a wide-ranging and suggestive coda, Fallon argues that after Elizabethan period, when authors used alter egos, they were always playing a metaliterary game. "As the author function solidified," Fallon writes, "the persona was reconceived in terms of self-reflexive irony, as a form of characteristically authorial metafiction" (154). It's possible to quibble with this chronology—the history of the picaresque, including the seventeenth-century craze for criminal "autobiographies," introduced more than one figure who could be described as a persona—but on the whole, I think Fallon is right. Later authors may have engaged in just as many self-conscious ironies as the Elizabethans, but they did so as a way of challenging the conventions of authorship rather than asserting them. It only remains to be seen whether, in a social and media environment that once more seems to be in flux, authorial categories will again transform. Will Karl Ove Knausgaard, like Philisides, wander into other autofictions?

Julianne Werlin is an assistant professor of English at Duke University. Her forthcoming book is titled *Writing at the Origin of Capitalism: Literary Circulation and Social Change in Early-Modern England.*

Book Review

LOUISE HORNBY

Cara Lewis, *Dynamic Form: How Intermediality Made Modernism*, Ithaca, NY: Cornell University Press, 2020.

Cara Lewis's *Dynamic Form: How Intermediality Made Modernism* proceeds from Virginia Woolf's ([1925] 1974: 173) provocation in her essay "Pictures" that a professor write a book called "The Loves of the Arts," which "would be concerned with the flirtations between music, letters, sculpture, and architecture, and the effects that the arts have had upon each other throughout the ages." Literature, Woolf claims, loves the hardest and widest of the arts, readily receiving impressions of sculpture, music, architecture, and painting throughout its history. Lewis situates literature's polyamory in modernism, asking, alongside Woolf, how it is that painting, sculpture, film, and photography make themselves felt in writing (2). Or, put a little differently, what does modernist literature love about visual and plastic art?

That modernist writing is in love with art is not questioned by Lewis or by Woolf. (We have plenty of books on that subject.) Rather, Lewis is interested in figuring out the terms and depths of such capacious love. For Lewis, the way art impresses itself upon literary form is not a matter of imitation but a matter of experience and feeling. Methodologically, this move is critical, for the shift from mimesis to feeling allows for her renewed investigation of modernism's formal commitments. Lewis argues alongside critics like David James that formalism

Genre, Vol. 54, No. 2   July 2021
DOI 10.1215/00166928-9263144   © 2021 by University of Oklahoma

is both modernism's legacy and its promise, for it is by attending to form that we encounter the political and social purchase of literature. Keeping in mind the expansive goals of the new modernist studies, Lewis aims to dissolve the association of modernism with what she calls "bad formalism"; that is, to break apart the conflation of modernism itself with aesthetic autonomy (Clive Bell's "significant form," New Criticism's strictures) (6). Rather than countering modernism's formalist tendencies with new historicism, as has been the field's bent, she endeavors to draw the new formalist studies alongside the new modernist studies, asking that formalism no longer be circumscribed by New Criticism's limits. Unbounded, "dynamic form" becomes the pivot for a consideration of what Lewis calls "intermediality," which, borrowing Woolf's terms, I understand to mean literature's various love affairs and dalliances with other arts.

   Dynamic Form is composed of five main chapters, each of which takes up a different formal proposition or offers a revision of a different "formal orthodoxy" by pairing an author with an art (13). The broad goal is to work through a set of received understandings about modernism—that modernist works are associated with "spatial form" (most famously argued by Joseph Frank), that modernism seeks pure or abstract form, and that modernism hews close (too close?) to formlessness. Lewis is more interested in pairing rather than paradigms: she brings narrative and time to bear on "spatial form" and stillness, finds the ground in abstraction, and form in dissolution. Her effort is not, however, to reinforce the either/or of these opposites but rather to locate the dynamism of form in the movement between terms and the interactions between media.

   The first chapter, "Plastic Form: Henry James's Sculptural Aesthetics and Reading in the Round," offers a sculptural reading of *The Golden Bowl*, which means both that Lewis pays close attention to the sculptural objects therein and that the encounter with sculpture in the novel teaches us something about how to read it "in the round." This chapter and the next are put to the task of resisting Frank's understanding of modernist narrative as spatial. Lewis wants to get at the experience of sculptural encounter as unfolding over time in incomplete circles and revolutions, which she sees as formative in James's novel. This chapter, like the others, is meticulously and carefully written, its readings of James nuanced, revealing over and over how *The Golden Bowl* loves sculpture. Even so, I am not sure that I am thoroughly convinced by the claim that sculptural viewing molds the formal perambulations of the reader of James's novel (although this is certainly true for the characters' movements). The metaphor that joins looking "in the round" at sculpture and reading elliptically dissolves in practice—even though they both unfold in time, the experience of walking around an object feels fundamentally different to that of reading a dense text.

From James's love of plastic form, Lewis moves in the second chapter to Woolf's desire for still life, focusing exclusively on Cézanne and *To the Lighthouse*. Lewis challenges received understandings of the still life's association with description rather than narration, looking to the ways in which the genre operates at the service of both by capturing the tensions between continuity and finitude, life and death. The chapter cleverly pivots away from positioning the painting at the center of the novel, Lily Briscoe's (not very good) abstract portrait, as its shaping force. Lewis points toward a different center—the bowl of fruit and seashell set carefully on the dinner table—her reading of which finds the novel's elegiac form in the still life, the genre that molds the terms of death and grief. Cézanne's still lives—his table arrangements—so central to Bloomsbury aesthetics, provide the chapter's correlative to the table's centerpiece. (Carol Armstrong's [2018] recent interdisciplinary scholarship on Cézanne would have been a welcome addition to Lewis's arguments about still life, Woolf, and Roger Fry's formalism.) Lewis gathers the novel's still life objects—folds of fabric, fruit, skulls, shells—which are also its discarded objects, those things left behind after a person has left the room or left the world. These still objects, which persist and move in time as well as space, are the forms that loss takes, providing the shape of the narrative to come.

The formal gravity (or groundedness) of the still life carries over into the next chapter, "Protean Form: Erotic Abstraction and Ardent Futurity in the Poetry of Mina Loy," which troubles modernist teleologies that see untethered abstraction as the apex of pure form. Loy's abstractions, shaped by Constantin Brancusi's sculptures, seek foundation and base physicality instead, muddying any notion of purity or formal completion. If the first three chapters are about literature's love of art and its objects, the encounters of the last two are more difficult to describe in terms of desire. Instead, they sound what feels more like a warning against loving film and photography, looking slightly askance while literature attempts to accommodate these "bad forms." The chapter on Waugh and film, "Bad Formalism: Evelyn Waugh's Film Fictions and the Work of Art in the Age of Cinematics," worries over the stakes of formal dissolution (formlessness) after film formalizes ephemerality and dynamism, and the final chapter, "Surface Forms: Photography and Gertrude Stein's Contact History of Modernism," considers photography's superficiality another "bad form" that undoes the forms of modernist writing. The arguments in each chapter are highly nuanced and would be of interest to scholars of either Waugh or Stein, but the general takeaway is this: the impermanence of film and the shallowness of photography make them bad forms for literature to love, as they threaten to erase form itself. This provocation returns *Dynamic Form* to its more broadly theoretical beginnings, which pull away from the finely tuned readings of the individual chapters to more general claims about form as object and method.

In the beginning and the end, then, what is form? To answer this, Lewis turns to Ali Smith's recent hybrid work, *Artful*, which I had just finished reading prior to writing this review. While I am aware that this coincidence means that its explanatory force might stand out in greater relief to me than other readers, Smith delivers a way to get at the intertwined stakes of love, feeling, and form that seem to be at the heart of *Dynamic Form*. Smith's *Artful* is a work of experimental literary criticism, a collection of four essays that are stitched together by a story of mourning and loss. It opens with grief's distended clock, "the twelve-month and a day" that has elapsed since the death of the unnamed narrator's lover (Smith 2012: 3). Even "more at a loss" than before, the narrator makes her way through the leftover lecture notes that remain piled on the dead lover's desk (another still life). This "unfinished stuff" provides the fluttery, incomplete structure for the four lecture/essays of the book, the second of which is titled "On Form." The notes for this lecture offer Lewis an expansive and modernist definition of form (resounding echoes of James Joyce throughout): "Form, from the Latin *forma*, meaning shape. Shape a mold; something that holds or shapes; a species or kind; a pattern or type; a way of being; order; regularity; system. It once meant beauty but now that particular meaning's obsolete. It means style and arrangement, structural unity in music, literature, painting, etc." (Smith 2012: 68; Lewis quotes this passage on p. 9). Form is, however, by no means fixed or prescriptive. Instead, as the lecture notes claim, form is both essential and protean, a shaper and shape-shifter, rule and its undoing. In Smith's (2012: 68) book, which negotiates the impermanence of the beloved, form begins to sound a lot like love, which has the capacity to "mold us" and "identify us" but whose hold is nonetheless tenuous or fleeting. As I understand it, the form of *Artless* is bereavement's excessive remaindering—the impressions left in the absence of another, a world that persists in emptiness.

Incomplete and changing, form does not create a sense of wholeness or comfort, and it is for this reason, I think, that Lewis turns, in the epilogue, to question
"form's ability to console" in the face of its own impermanence (220). I was not
anticipating this turn to consolation at the end and indeed might not be able to
square it with the intricacies of the rest of the work without help from Smith. *Artful*'s narrator seeks solace in form but does so with no expectation that the loss
of the beloved be repaired. Instead, small comfort is gleaned from form. Lewis
quotes Smith (2012: 77) in her final paragraph (229): "In its apparent fixity, form
is all about change. In its fixity, form is all about the relationship of change to
continuance, even when the continuance is itself precarious." While Lewis stops
there, I read want to read further in Smith (2012: 77), who follows with a poetic
example of continuance's precarity:

> here, for instance, fragility *and* its opposite sureness are evident in the form,
> the diminishing line-length, and the thematic preoccupation of Wisława Szym-
> borska's six-line poem (translated by Cavanagh and Barańczak) called, simply,
> "Vermeer."
> > So long as that woman from the Rijksmuseum
> > in painted quiet and concentration
> > keeps pouring milk day after day
> > from the pitcher to the bowl
> > the World hasn't earned
> > the world's end.

This is a solacing poem, but it does not console with a false promise of formal
wholeness. Instead, the receding lines map the tension between ongoingness (the
present imperfect tense of "pouring") and anticipated finitude (the world will
eventually end). It vouches thus for a still persistence that is constituted by eventual loss. Yet the suggestion that an oil painting might offer the only evidence
that the world has not, in fact, ended is to say that the world already has—it just
didn't earn it.

I include the poem here because it acts as Ockham's razor, sharpening my
understanding of Lewis's argument that modernist form gives shape to the incomplete promise of change, allowing for its dynamism. Its dynamism—its force—is
the strength of form's love to carry from one object to another. Literature's love
for other arts is not just a starting point but an essential condition of modernist
form. Elaborated thus, the conclusions that Lewis draws in *Dynamic Form* are
deeply compelling and even consoling as they recuperate form for modernist
studies and reanimate conversations about the relationship between the arts.

Louise Hornby is associate professor of English at the University of California, Los Angeles. She is the author of *Still Modernism: Photography, Literature, Film* (2017). She is currently working on a project about the visual culture of weather in the twentieth century.

Works Cited

Armstrong, Carol. 2018. *Cézanne's Gravity*. New Haven, CT: Yale University Press.
Smith, Ali. 2012. *Artful*. London: Hamish Hamilton.
Woolf, Virginia. (1925) 1974. *The Moment and Other Essays*. New York: Harcourt.